Hello and welcome to the journey of my life! My name is Marti'ka Strong, and I was born and raised in Rock Hill, South Carolina. I am a mother of 2 boys, a business owner, a daughter, sister, cousin, and a friend! I decided to write No More Broken Pieces because I was broken. I have experienced so much hurt and pain throughout my 31 years of living, that I refused to live this way forever.

I was a victim, I caused pain, I did some hurtful things, but I was hurting. The only things that truly saved me was God, my kids, and writing. I no longer wanted to live in my past but in my future. I have always been a big dreamer and I knew that whatever I was going through at that moment was temporary, so I had to find a way out.

Some of the stories shared here are only just a few of my life changing events, but they made me better. So, I encourage you that as you read each chapter to look within yourself and find you if you haven't already!

God Bless!

No More Broken Pieces

By: Marti'ka Strong

No More Broken Piece

Copyright © 2021 by Marti'ka Strong.

All rights reserved. No part of this book may be reproduced or transmitted in any form or by any means without written permission from the author.

Scriptures marked KJV are taken from the King James Version (KJV). Copyright

ISBN - 978-0-578-90344-6

Acknowledgement

Eureka Hyman Photography

'Capturing the beauty of your journey'

www.eureka-hyman.com

Instagram: eureka_hyman

Thank you for capturing beautiful photos for me!!!!

Anitra Meeks for editing and making sure everything was complete!

I love you ladies and thank you for helping make my book a reality!

Table of Contents

Dedication **8**

Realization **9**

Introduction **11**

The Road to Self-Discovery **13**

No More Running **14**

Section One: From A Girl to A Women **18**
1.1: Pieces of the Puzzle 19
1.2: The Start of It All 21
1.3: We Are Sisters: Not Enemies 25
1.4: A Mother's Love 28
1.5: That's Not My Name 31
1.6: Know Who You Are 33

Section Two: Revelation of the Flesh **35**
2.1: Making Wrong Choices 36
2.2: Sex Shouldn't Be The Only Factor 38
2.3: Lustful Desire: My Flesh Wants What It Wants 41
2.4: You Want To Be Grown 44
2.5: Children Out Of Wedlock: Teenage Motherhood 48
2.6: Why the Health Department Calling Me 55
2.7: You Tested Positive 57
2.8: Loneliness: Why Do I Feel So Alone 59
2.9: You Not Ready 63
2.10: Don't Write A Check You Can't Cash 68
2.11: Never Make A Friend Because You Lonely 73
2.12: Bad Habits Can Corrupt Your Character 76

Section 3: Mental Battles and Silent Tears **79**
3.1: Battlefield Of The Mind 80

3.2: Why You Mad? 83
3.3: The Unspoken Truth 85
3.4: Just Kill Yourself Already 86
3.5: Thank God For Your Judas 89
3.6: The Hole 91
3.7: 6 Plus "One" 95
3.8: Knowing When To Let Go 99
3.9: Stop Holding On 101
3.10: Healing Is Required 104
3.11: Fading Vision 105
3.12: Me vs Me 109

Section Four: I Must Fight! My Destiny Is On The Line..115
Explosive Desire 116

4.1: The Skies Has No Limits 120
4.2: My Dreams Shall Come True 122
4.3: I Dream Like Him 124
4.4: My Dreams Show Me Things 126
4.5: The Courage To Stand 129
4.6: I Need Courage Spiritually Too..................................130
4.7: I Had To Graduate 133
4.8: Dedication Is Important 136
4.9: I Made It Baby 137
4.10: My Dedication Is Not In Vain 140
4.11: Success Isn't Overnight 142
4.12: I See My Success..143
4.13: Success Comes By Hearing 145

Section Five: Spiritual Growth: My Flesh Can't Win Forever 147

5.1: Prayer Changes Things ……………………………………..148
5.2: Prayer Has Changed Me ……………………………...149
5.3: Prayer Healed Me Last Night ……………………….152
5.4: Jesus Wasn't An Option …………………………….154
5.5: The Perfect Remedy ……………………………………156
5.6: I Need Jesus…………………………………………………...157
5.7: Woman After God's Heart………………………………160
5.8: Giving Should Be Natural ……………………………….162
5.9: I Can Help Them ……………………………………………164
5.10: Forgiveness ……………………………………………………168
5.11: Jesus Can Do It All …………………………………………170
5.12: Acceptance ……………………………………………………172
5.13: A Queen's Decree …………………………………………173
The End ……………………………………………………………….175
Special Prayer ……………………………………………………..177

Dedication

I dedicate this book to my middle school counselor, Debbie Cabiness, for being there during one of the toughest times in my life. She was always available to encourage me, lift me up, and offer a shoulder to lean on when I needed advice or someone to talk to. She was full of the motherly love I was missing and needed. She showed me that my heart is filled with love and taught me to never give up, or never to allow my circumstances or fears to stop me from reaching for the stars. From her I learned that one person can make a difference in the lives of many.

So, I dedicate my book to Mrs. Cabiness because she truly opened my eyes to life. Thank you for everything, and I love you very much. Please continue to touch other people's lives like you did mine!

By the grace of God, I say thank you to my mother, Althea Mann, for always making sure my kids and I have never gone without. We love you! Thank you Shantina Gilliam, for being a sister who always pushes me to be better and fight no matter what. And Prince Blackmon, thank you for encouraging me to write this book.

And finally, thanks to all my family, friends, and all other people who have supported me, inspired me, and just loved me along my journey in life.

Giving God praise and glory for His love, support, guidance, and forgiveness.

God Bless!

Realization

As I wrote this book, a part of me wanted to leave out some of the pieces that broke me. I didn't want to discredit someone else life or make someone else look bad. I just needed to tell my story. Every story has 3 side: your side, their side, and the truth.

I wanted to show the world how God can do something with broken pieces. How He took my broken pieces and made me whole while giving me life during the process. I don't blame God nor people for anything I have faced. I had and still have a choice in how things were done and is being done in my life. Yet I also know that if God allowed me to endure in it, it was for a reason.

Yes! Some of the things that has happened to me were out of my control. But I learned and understand better that our warfare isn't carnal. We fight not against flesh and blood but of spirits in high places. We are all spirits that are host in a body. Some people have good spirits while some have bad spirits. But, at the end of the day, this daily battle has nothing to do with you or me. And no matter how bad we want answers to life or may think we may know all the answers, somethings will be left unanswered.

I said all that to say, I'm telling my story through physical and spiritual eyes. I have learned spiritually that it wasn't the actual person that I though was after me. It was the actual spirits that were attached to the person. Some spirits are attached or assigned to a certain person that they may not even be aware of.

Instead of being mad at a person, pray against the spirits that are attached to that person. And yes, it's okay to forgive and love a person from a distance. So, I am asking that as you read my story that you will try to see it through spiritual eyes. That you read with no judgment, but to see the lesson in each story told.

There is no way possible to overcome anything if you CAN'T, DON'T, WON'T learn how to look through different lenses.

Please know that this book was not written in a specific order. These are stories that has occurred throughout my life

Introduction

Have you ever experienced a pain so deep during your childhood that it caused you to feel shame or less than what you really are? As each year pass you by, you push it into the back of your heart and mind. Never taking the time to fully deal with it. Convincing yourself and others that you are ok, but you aren't. Because you never took the time to deal with it, you told yourself that it will eventually go away.

Constantly fighting a battle that you felt no longer existed or even mattered. Making certain decision throughout your life based off what occurred during your childhood. Causing you more hurt and pain over the years.

I can be the first to admit that used to be me. As a child, God revealed my destiny to me. I knew that I had a great future ahead of me, but the hurt of my past followed me as I got older. Making choices from my past hurt and leaving me with the feelings of never reaching my destiny. But I knew it was all a lie because I believed God for the vision, He gave me.

My destiny was calling me but to reach it, I had to rewind back to my childhood and deal with some pains. I had to tackle every pain from childhood and even the other pains I caused along the way. Those pains of yesterday were draining me, and I could no longer hold on. I had to deal with it to move ahead.

Everything you're going through or went through happened for a reason. See, God already knows our lives, but we do not. We know the day we entered this world but not the day we will leave. Because of this, we must trust in God to guide us. At the same time, we must daily decide how we are going to live. We must learn how to truly let go of the past to reach the future.

I understand that some things are easier said than done. However, it is time to realize that whatever you do or do not accomplish in life is your responsibility. No one can stop you from reaching your destiny, except you.

Life is not easy, but God will carry you the whole way if you allow Him too. *No More Broken Pieces* was written to encourage you to tackle your past pains and fight for your tomorrow. This book will encourage and help you to tackle the challenges in your life, so you can truly move on to the next chapter of your life. In order to do that you must read this book with a spirit of willingness and honesty. Read and understand this book because love and truth play a major part of your life.

God Bless!

The Road to Self-Discovery

Never be afraid to discover who you are!!!!!!

(Thursday March 23, 2017)

No More Running

Boom! Boom! Boom!

Looking out the window in my room to see if there was a car outside, rolling my eyes, I sat back down on my bed to finish listening to my sister talk on the phone. She was giving me some tips on what I needed to do to be approved for a mortgage.

Boom! Boom! Boom!

Hopping up to walk into the living room only to look again through the blinds. After seeing him standing there, I was hesitant to answer the door; I no longer cared about what he had to say or how he felt. I was completely over the entire situation. Three more knocks came, along with the ring of the doorbell. I finally opened the door to let him know I was on the phone, except none of that mattered. He forced himself into my house and walked past me to the bathroom.

I was no longer in the mood to hear about fixing my credit. My gut was telling me something was about to happen, and it was not going to be good. He started texting and calling early this morning. Mad because he was busted, and I was not answering my phone. Regardless of if they had sex or not, I caught on to the game quick and was done. I no longer wanted what we started almost four months ago. His level of disrespect was real high.

I told my sister, "Aye! I love you, but let me call you back," wishing I wouldn't have opened the door. She told me she loved me as well and we hung up. My spirit was telling me to text her to call 911 and send them to my house, but I did not. I ignored it and walked into my room.

No more than three minutes passed before he started running off at the mouth. Scrolling through my phone with no worries at the time, he snatched the phone out my hand and said, "Erase my number out your phone!" He walked in the other direction, trying to open my phone.

I responded, "For your information sir, your number been deleted out my phone." I reached for my phone only to be pushed with a force.

"Move man! I'm about to delete all our text messages out the phone." he stated.

"No, you not! Give me my phone." I reached for my phone again.

"Move! You aren't getting nothing." he said as he pushed me again.

Reaching for my phone for the third time, I swung as he attempted to push me away again. Not sure where I hit him at, he said "F*** you and your phone!" Throwing the phone onto the floor, he stomped on it, completely shattering the screen.

Next thing I know I was in a headlock and he was trying to choke the life out of me. I reached for my dresser, knocking stuff down on the floor. I needed something to hit him with to get him off me. There were some red pliers in reach. The same red plies he used to hook up my washer machine 3 weeks before. I hit him with in the face to loosen his grip around my neck.

Attempting to gain composure, I looked down at my feet and notice I was missing a sock. The coldness of the floor made me think about the coldest of his heart.

"B****, you made me bleed."

No longer standing toe to toe with him, I slipped, and he attacked me like I had really done something to him. Like a lion attacking its prey. Kicking me. Punching me. Kicking me. Punching me. Over and over again.

Every time I attempted to get up, I was kicked back down. Looking into those brown, bold eyes that I once fallen in love with. I no longer saw love in his eyes, but now the look of rage. The look of "I will really kill you." I asked him was it really that serious to go to jail for murder.

Another punch to my body; it must have been that serious because he started choking me again. His grip was so strong; I begin losing consciousness. I felt myself giving up. I slightly turned my head to the right to bite his arm enough to loosen his grip. It worked. I thought I was finally free but, he came back with an even tighter grip.

No longer at the end of the bed, I had to fight to get away, but I did not make it far before he grabbed me tighter, pushing me to the middle of the bed. He tried to break my neck. Luckily, the upper part of my body was slowing turning in the same direction, so he could not get the grip he needed.

I felt myself grasping for air as my eyes begin to close. My life. My children. Everything started flashing before my eyes. I no longer had the energy to fight; I no longer had the strength to hold on. So, I called out to Jesus in my mind "Lord it's not my time to die."

I felt his body lift off me enough for me to come underneath him. We tussled for a little more before I was able to break free. Running out the front door, with one sock on, half ripped shirt, and blood everywhere, looking for help. I was now running for my life in my own home.

God had given me multiply warnings before this event occurred. I was not trying to hear what God was saying. I wanted to do what Marti'ka wanted to do. I was being disobedient in so many ways and I knew it. You know how the saying goes, "When you know better you, do better". Well, I knew better and chose not to do better.

There was no way to deny the truth because I knew it. I was warned enough times to walk away before and during the moments when I felt like pleasing my flesh. At the time, pleasing my flesh was more important than what was best for me.

As a young mother of two boys, I needed to know how I ended up here. Deciding to please my flesh instead of pleasing God almost cost me my life but why. Disobedience to God played a major role in me landing here but the question I had to ask myself was "Why am I being disobedient?"

It was now time to truly evaluate my life to see why I kept making the same choices repeatedly. Why I kept settling for less when I am the daughter of the Most High God! I just did not understand but there was no more time to be wasted it was now time to figure it out and know the truth behind it. It was now time to dig deep into the root causes of it all.

Either you will allow your childhood to make you or break you.

-Marti'ka Strong

Section One:

From A Girl to A Women

Don't allow your childhood to be your adulthood!

1.1: Pieces of the Puzzle

Life is like a puzzle and in every puzzle no two pieces are the same. Some pieces are straight or round. While others are jagged, pointed, and curvy. Putting piece by piece together, the puzzle will become complete.

Well, that's life. Each piece of your life makes a complete picture of who you are. You cannot take a small piece and put it beside a big piece if it does not fit. Instead, you must take the piece that fits. Bit by bit and piece by piece until that picture is complete.

For many years, I always tried to tell a piece of my puzzle without including all the pieces. Once I decided to add all the pieces to my story from the small to the big, I realized that my picture was starting to become complete.

Who I am today did not just start with the abandonment of my father or losing my grandparents! It was a combination of my father, my mother, my sister, and losing two important people in my life, my grandparents.

As I reflect on my childhood and going down the road of forgiveness, I realize I can never reach my purpose if I am not willing to speak on all the pieces to my puzzle. I was trying to skip some pieces only to realized that it was because I was still hurt by them. I was not alone. I was not the only one that had experienced these hurts and pain. Some people just aren't willing and ready to talk about those pieces that hurt them the most.

I can't encourage you to answer the phone to your destiny when I was hesitated to answer my own call. I had to open and talk about it all to truly reach the finish line.

My puzzle was only complete when I finally decided to deal with it all.

    Complete your puzzle by adding all the pieces. The hurtful, the happy, the good, the bad, and the ugly. All your pieces so that you may be complete and reach your destiny. Your destiny is calling you, so I dare you to answer it.

1.2: The Start of It All

(Let's rewind back to 1998. My 2nd grade year at Ebinport Elementary)

"Okay class, please quiet down. I have a new assignment for everyone to do. Does everyone remember the problem I went over yesterday before the end of class?" Mrs. Smith asked as she started passing out the new assignment to the class.

"Now class please."

There was a slight tap at the door.

"Please excuse me." Mrs. Smith told the class as she walked toward the door.

"Yes, may I help you?" Asking the two gentleman that were standing at the door. I wasn't sure who the gentlemen were, but they were wearing some green uniforms that I had never seen before.

"Hello Mrs. Smith. How are you doing today? My name is Sergeant Strong, and this is Lieutenant Cape. I am here to see my daughter Marti'ka Strong before I leave back out. I am currently on active duty and I don't know when I will be returning." The gentlemen stated as he was giving Mrs. Smith a handshake.

"I'm sure she will be excited to see you!" Exclaimed Mrs. Smith as she turned to call my name.

"Marti'ka, you have a surprise visitor at the door." I heard the excitement in Mrs. Smith voice, but I wasn't sure if I was supposed to be excited with her. Getting up from the desk, I walked toward the door, wondering who was coming to visit me that was a man. I didn't know where my daddy was, so I felt it couldn't have been him.

"Daddy!" I screamed and ran towards him as soon as I realized it really was my daddy. I haven't seen my daddy or talked to him in a long time. All I wanted was for him to come back home.

"Hey baby!" He said as he embraced his baby girl with open arms. Hugging him as tight as I could I didn't want to ever let go. I really missed my daddy.

"Daddy, I don't want you to leave. I really miss you. Please don't leave me again." I pleaded for my daddy not to leave while still embracing him. But I knew that would never happen. Whoever this man was with him was going to make sure he left me again.

Grabbing my hand, he asked me where my desk was, so I could show him all the things I had learned in the 2nd grade. Walking towards the back of the class,

"This is my desk daddy. Right here in the very back." I said pointing at my desk.

Sitting down to attempt to show him what I was currently learning in Math, there was something in the back of my mind that wouldn't let me enjoy the moment. I knew he had to leave, and I felt I wasn't good enough to make him stay.

"Daddy, look at this problem. Five times five is twenty-five. Let me show you how that's the answer!"

Showing my daddy on paper using tally marks, the gentlemen with him interrupted me to let him know that it was now time to go.

"I'm sorry but it's time," he said with a deep voice that was full of power and authority. My eyes were now full of tears because he was taking my daddy away from me again.

"Marti'ka baby, I want you to be all you can be no matter what. Know that daddy loves you with every bone within me!" He told me hugging me once again before he kissed me on the forehead.

"I love you Marti'ka. Never forget that!" He told me once again before he turned to walk toward the door.

"Thank you, Mrs. Smith!" My daddy said before he looked into my eyes one last time.

"You welcome." Mrs. Smith told my daddy as he walked out the door and she slowly closed the door behind her.

No longer concerned with the assignment Mrs. Smith had just gave the class, I started concerning myself with everything else to take my focus off the fact my daddy was gone out my life again. Mrs. Smith approach me with concern in her eyes. "Marti'ka are you ok baby?"

"I guess I will be fine. He always walks out my life." I said with sorrow in my voice. I no longer wanted to be at school. I now wanted to go home and crawl in my bed. Looking into my small brown eyes Mrs. Smith told me that everything will be fine. But instead of listening to what she was saying, I pulled out my glue and put it all over the desk and my hands. At that very moment, I felt my life was crumbling before my eyes. Not even realizing that my life was just beginning.

Abandonment is a hurt that I don't wish on no one. It's a feeling that's very indescribable, yet at some point in our lives we may experience it. Rather it's your father, your mother, a friend, or even in a relationship, it may happen.

Due to experiencing abandonment around the age of 7, I felt unloved, unworthy, and not good enough for my father. I felt that if my father abandoned me that no one really loved me even though I had my family there to love me. I begin to doubt me as a person, and I desired to have that love in my life. Not even realizing that this desire was about to take me on a roller coaster in life.

1.3: We Are Sisters: Not Enemies

The relationship between my sister and I growing up was like mixing oil and vinegar together. We never mixed. Growing up in the same house, sharing the same purple room was like living in a prison cell with a person you just met for the first time.

I knew my sister loved me. We shared the same mother but then there were times I wasn't sure. During certain points in my life, I questioned the bond we had and how we would always fuss and fight.

Growing up raising ourselves after our grandparents passed, was the time we should have grew closer together, instead we grew apart. I knew that if I ever needed her, she was there, but we didn't have a bond where we could talk about everything. Instead, over the years we grew apart. She chose to bond with my cousin and others instead.

I felt like my sister had abandoned me for my cousin and neglected me. There were times when she would intentionally try to hurt me or mistreat me for no reason. I know that siblings' fuss and fight but there were times when I felt like my sister wanted to take me out. Better yet, that I didn't even exist.

The moment that changed my view of our relationship my entire teenage years and mostly my twenties, was when she told me that she didn't want to go to a party with me. Her reason for it was because no one liked me. The opinion of others mattered to her more than I did. I didn't have many friends and a lot of females didn't like me, but I was her sister. They weren't her sister, and they didn't share the same blood that we did. So why did their feelings matter to her more than mine did?

Despite all the other things she did to me, I felt at that very moment, I no longer had a big sister. She had now become someone I just shared a room with that always judged me. I instantly put a wall up against her, not letting her into my life. Whenever she did ask a question or try to talk, I would only give her pieces but never the complete story. There would also be time that I just wouldn't talk at all.

My sister's actions toward me caused me to resist my family and run to the streets. There I thought I could find someone to keep it real with me and accept me for who I am. I felt if my sister who I shared the same blood with didn't love me then my family didn't love me either.

I blamed my sister for years on how she treated me, resisting her in a lot of ways. Walking around with a wall up against her but also making it harder to let others in as well. Talking at times and saying I love you but only because it was the right thing to do. Not because it was truly genuinely and 100 percent real. Until one day, I started seeing certain similar behaviors in my boys I experienced growing up. That's when I realized I could no longer walk around with un-forgiveness in my heart toward my sister.

As a mother and knowing the hurt and neglect from my past, I didn't want my boys to experience the same things I did. I needed them to be closer than we were and have a bond that no one could ever break. It was now time to break this curse over my family. I had to stop the enemy's plan. I could no longer allow this pain and hurt to move down to my children. It was now time to fight and forgive. Fight for my kids tomorrow but also forgive for my tomorrow.

I had to completely let go of the hurt of the past and work toward being a better Marti'ka for them and myself. History can and will only repeat itself in a family if you allow it too.

Overall, despite everything my sister and I been through, she never told me anything wrong. Regardless of how she may have said it, there was always truth to it. My sister always seen things in me that I didn't always see. I learned that she always wanted me to value myself and others as well. And to never settle for nothing but the best.

So, I encourage you to forgive if you have ever experience hurt or neglect from a sibling. Don't allow that same hurt, pain, or neglect pass down to your children or children's children. No matter how you feel that someone may have impacted your life in a hurtful way, don't allow the situation to have control over you. You control the situation by forgiving and more forward with your life with love.

No one should control your emotions, only you should have control over your emotions. Family should be important, but you can't control how a person feel or think about you. Only you can reach your destiny, but you must learn how to forgive to reach it.

1.4: A Mother's Love

It was Valentine's Day morning, my brother, sister, and I woke up to a box of chocolate, a small teddy bear, and a balloon that said, "I love you" for each one of us. It was gift from our mother, letting us know she loved us and to enjoy our day. And even though she was absent a lot, she always made sure we were good. No love is as precious as a mother's love.

My mother was the general manager at McDonald's at the time and as much as I knew she loved all her children. To me, McDonald's was her first family. My mother worked hard every day to provide for us. Growing up with every materialistic item that a child could have or ask for. Wearing name brand clothes, shoes, updated electronics, and getting a car when it was time to drive.

Still, her presence was missing. She worked so much that she didn't have time to help with homework or time for the small mother daughter talks. When I was going through things in life, she wasn't there to direct or comfort me. Work and sleep were all she knew. Sleep and work. So, growing up as a young lady, I was raising myself.

I made sure that my mother came home every day to a clean home and sometimes I would cook breakfast or dinner just for us to eat. Watching my mother slave for a billion-dollar company, I promise myself that I would never allow myself to be like her. I would never allow myself to give up on my dream. I would never settle for the highest position in a company that was never mine just to provide for my children.

Every day after school, I would do my homework and study for my test if I had any to take. If there was something I didn't understand in class, I made sure that the teacher gave me a better understanding, so I could pass. I never wanted to disappoint my mother because I knew she worked hard for us to have the world. I wanted her to always be proud of me with no regrets because she gave up on her dreams for us to live.

Unfortunately, along the path of life, I became a teenage mother in which she didn't see for me at that time. I was trying to live my life to meet my mother expectation, but this was a choice I had to do for me. I had to follow my heart. I became a mother younger than she did. But through it all, she was my strongest support system.

She might not have been the mother I needed growing up, but she was the mother I needed when I became a mother. A mother's love can never be replaced. I questioned some of her choices growing up, but I learned a lot from her along the way.

I used to be broken because there were times, I needed her the most and she wasn't there. I blamed her job from taking her away from us. From me. For never allowing her to be the mother I needed her to be. I felt if she were there more, I wouldn't never have made certain choices in my life. And the times I was so rebellious, I wouldn't have been.

Until I sat back and reflected over my life. I asked myself would I be as strong as I am if she was there? Would I know how to fight for my destiny ahead?

Because of her absence, I learned and pushed myself to stand. I learned how to fight for my dreams without accepting failure as an option. It hasn't been easy and to say I haven't thought about giving up would be a lie. Then something slaps me in the face to remind me of my mother choice to stop dreaming and for me to never stop running. Giving up isn't an option and I truly thank her for that.

1.5: That's Not My Name

I grew up in a small city call Rock Hill where everybody knew just about everybody. Unfortunately, for my small city, the hate was real. I must admit growing up, I had my messy, disrespectful, nasty, sluttish, crazy, and spiteful moments. But I was just a young girl trying to figure out life and live my life to the fullest.

I was a fortunate young girl who lacked nothing materialistically. My momma made sure we had nice things even to this day. I was about 5'1 weighting about 139 pounds with absolutely no stomach. I was caramel complexion, beautiful with a gorgeous bright smile. I had one of the baddest shapes in Rock Hill in my younger days. (Believe me there was a lot of attention that I wasn't seeking for).

My personality on the other hand was wild. I was very loud and outspoken. Quick to speak before I think, and my body language used to always tell on me. Even though I was very blunt, I was a loving, outgoing, and full of energy type of person.

Along my journey in life, I have been called every name in the world that you can call someone. I got along with dudes so easily that the dudes loved me, but the females couldn't stand the ground I walked on. Most of the name calling came from the females but there were a few dudes that did as well.

People don't realize that words really do carry a form of weight on people. When I was in elementary, I was called pie face and long lip because of the structure of my head and my bottom lip hung. I was also called s*** face because of the birth mark upon my lip. And on top of that, I was always told I could not talk because my English was improper.

When I hit middle school, I became a "slut", "rude", and "nasty". By the time I hit high school, I was every word that you could think of.

I started battling with self-esteem issues in elementary because I was picked on. I didn't understand at the time I was created perfectly in God's image. My face was flat, my lip was long. I had a birthmark above my lip and my speech was not the best. And to top it off, I wore by focus glasses. Shortly, labeled something I really was not because no one really took the time to get to know me. It wasn't my fault that all the dudes were looking and wanted me. I really was not that girl that had sex with every dude I gave my number too. I grew up with a lot of unnecessary attention that I really didn't care for.

On the outside looking in, they were hating because all the men wanted me but, in the inside, I was dealing with self-esteem issues. I was learning how to love and accept Marti'ka for who she was. Regardless of the different name calling and experience, I told myself that I am not what they call me. I am what and who God has called me to be. It doesn't matter what the next person says or label you as. The question, is who do you believe you are?

Look at your name. What do you see? Do you know what your name stands for?

1.6: Know Who You Are

Your name is a significant part of your life, regardless of whether you like your name or not. Most names come from historical and linguistic origins with meaning already attached to them. Even if your name doesn't have a meaning, you can create your own meaning and live by that.

Marti'ka Sharday Strong is my name. Marti'ka doesn't carry any meaning at all, while Sharday means "runaway." Strong means being able to withstand great force or pressure. I most definitely stand behind my last name and the things I have accomplished and overcame. So here is the introduction to me: I am Marti'ka Sharday Strong, and welcome to my world!

Marvelous
Adorable
Remarkable
Truthful
Intelligent
'-(breath)
Kind
Amazing

Spontaneous
Hustler
Ambitious
Respectable
Determined
Adventurous
Young

Strong
Talented
Real
Outstanding
Nice
Gorgeous

So, what do all these words mean? For starters, I am marvelous, adorable, and remarkable in all my ways. I am very truthful and intelligent, reaching out to touch and change many people's lives. Hold on, wait! I need to catch my breath! I am also kind and amazing, willing, and ready to share everything that I have discovered so far in life.

While I am very spontaneous with my ideas, I will continue to hustle until I can't anymore. I am ambitious enough to reach higher than the stars and respectable enough to earn my dreams. Determined despite my fears, uncertainty, and worries, I am very adventurous and young and so ready to face the ups and downs of life.

I am strong, standing firm and tall behind my last name. I am blessed and talented, with so much to accomplish. The love I have to give is real and greater than I can understand. And to top it off, I am outstanding, nice, and gorgeous. Marti'ka Sharday Strong is the name, and I don't play any games.

Know who you are and understand what your name stands for, even if you create that meaning yourself. Make sure that you love and know who you are!

Everyone has their own giants to face in life. No matter how big the giant may look. Know that every giant must fall.

---Marti'ka Strong

Section Two:

Revelations of the Flesh

Personal growth comes from personal experience.

2.1: Making Wrong Choices

Regardless of how hard I may try to live the right way in life, I will just admit it, I'm far from perfect. I have made plenty of mistakes with plenty more to come. I am sure of, only because I am human. Along my path of mistakes that I made, it made me weak and sensitive to a lot of things. Choices I would regret and choices I would learn from.

I made the wrong choices based off what has happened to me in the past. I was searching to try to find answers and fill a void, only ending up in a hole or up against the wall. Soon regretting the choice that I made. I was trying to find the answer, but I found more hurt instead.

So, let's look at the definition of wrong choices and how it can impact life and the people attached to you as well:

- not correct or true.
- unjust, dishonest, or immoral.
- in an unsuitable or undesirable manner or direction.

You must learn to be aware of your choices and the words you use. "The tongue of the just is as choice silver: the heart of the wicked is little worth." (Proverbs 10:20)

I have made plenty of choices that affected me later in life. Whether it was in 2 days, 2 weeks, 2 months, or 2 years, that choice came back to help or hinder me. When I make wrong choices, I end up facing obstacles I didn't have to face. This is especially true when there was a sign to either warn or stop me.

Life is a journey that must fight its course but along the way I learned that I can be renewed. Psalm 51:10 states

"Create in me a clean heart, O God; and renew a right spirit within me." So, I know making the wrong choice today doesn't always determine my tomorrow but if I neglect the truth of my heart, it can.

Life sometimes made me feel like I was less then what I really am, especially when I made the wrong choices. For example, there has been a time when I felt like if my choice is private and I'm not bothering anybody else, what's the problem? But even the most personal, well-meant decisions can have serious consequences for myself and others in life.

One of the worst decisions I ever made was having sex before marriage. It caused many confusing and painful experiences. While I am not married yet, the good does outweigh the bad for me; I have grown a lot over the years. However, I pray that, after hearing my story, you will understand why I believe having sex before marriage is the wrong choice to make. If you haven't had sex yet, here are a few reasons why I believe you should wait until marriage.

2.2: Sex Shouldn't Be The Only Factor

It was a typically Friday night and I had just got home from a cookout with the girls. My boyfriend and I met up at my house to have sex, but I was in my feelings.

"Who was that girl you were talking to with that pink dress on?" I asked him with curiosity in my voice!

"What girl with the pink dress on?" He responded with a confused look on his face.

"Man. Stop playing with me. You were talking to her for a long time! Let me guess, that was another one of your cousins from your daddy side, huh?" Responding with an attitude.

"Marti'ka, you know I have a lot of family around here so go head with asking me questions about other females. You already know what's going on between us anyways!" He said as grabbed me and started kissing my neck.

I love when he kisses on my neck, and I was already intoxicated from drinking at the cookout. I looked passed the lie he had just told me and allowed myself to let loose. It was time to have some fun in the bedroom that I would come back to this conversation later!

Have you ever been in a relationship that you knew wasn't healthy for you, but you stayed involved in it because of the sex? Deep down inside you knew he wasn't the one for you. You soon become a victim to his lies and games.

You start telling yourself that he will stop lying to you and he really does love you. You decide to stay only to be left for one of the girls he was cheating on you with.

You're left wondering why you stayed and why you cared so much about him. You even start to question your self-worth, self-love, and even your sex abilities.

When you have sexual encounter with a man, a soul tie is created. Sex open doors that determine if a person stays or goes in tight situations. When you are attached, you allow yourself to stick around even when you know leaving is the best decision. Your actions are now based off sexual encounters instead of reality. You believe that he loves you because of the sex, but nothing else is adding up.

Have you ever made a choice based off your sexual relationship with someone? You wanted him to be the one, so you wouldn't have to be alone or start over again. Or maybe, you were just running from the truth about yourself.

If anyone is looking for an example of someone who has made this mistake, just pick me. I know all about it and the pain that will come with it. Life is a journey so along that journey comes lessons. Those mistakes are your lessons. Either you will learn and grow from them or you will let it break you.

You are killing yourself slowly inside because you refuse to be honest with yourself? You know that isn't love. Whether you grew up in an environment where lies are constantly being told or not, you know when something makes you feel good or bad. If the person makes you smile, laugh, and brings out the good in you, then that is love! If the person makes you cry, causes pain, and only hinders you from growing, then you know that isn't love.

I have learned that I was lying to myself to ignore the pain I was really experiencing. I just didn't want to deal with it, so I pushed it away and allowed the true issue at hand to linger around like flies as life was passing me by. But this is not how God wishes for me to live or you either. Not to lie is a commandment that was given by Him, and I believe in my heart that it applies to me lying to myself as well. Trying to make myself feel better. Regardless of my intentions or feelings, lying is a sin even when I'm lying to myself.

If you are someone who constantly lies to yourself, God has already spoken over your life. He already knows what He has in store for you. So, there's no need to lie to yourself to convince yourself you are loved when God has already called you His son or daughter. He has already offered you loved. Be free in Jesus and be honest with yourself about everything. The more you are honest, the more you will live. I need God in everything that I do, and that includes being honest with myself.

Choices like having sex before marriage can lead to consequences so painful that it will make you develop a wall against people and good things in life. These incorrect choices can send your mind spinning in doubt and fear. Wrong choices bring sadness that no one wants to experience but God's love, can lift you up and bring you out of your sorrows.

So, I encourage you to look within yourself and face the reality of who you are. You must find out why you make the decision to settle. Why do you allow yourself to fight for someone else instead of fighting for yourself? Why do you allow yourself to keep lying if you are? You must be willing to figure out the root cause of it all.

2.3: Lustful Desire:

My Flesh Wants What It Wants

"Girl did you just see that light skin dude with the braids over there near the gym?" I was talking to my best friend, standing outside of A building waiting on class to start. It was the 2nd semester of our 9th grade year and I was single. I was so single and ready to mingle. I was fresh out of a relationship and was ready for the new high school boys' journey.

"No! Where he at girl?" she asked as she started looking around to see what I was seeing.

"Girl, right there with Michelle ugly self." I was no longer talking with excitement in my voice, instead my motives changed very fast. In two seconds, I went from happy to disappoint because he was talking to her. But none of that mattered. I was determined to have him regardless.

So, I know you probably wondering what I mean when I say my motives changed in two seconds huh? Well, Michelle was in my English class and I didn't like her. It was clear and obvious that she didn't like me either. She walked around like it was all about her, swinging her hair and smacking her lips. Walking with her nose in the air like someone owed her something.

So, I decided to make a move on the dude anyways. She wasn't my friend, and we didn't like each other. On top of that, I was already looking before I seem them talking.

I slowly made my way in with a bright smile and looking into his eyes. I asked about her when we started talking but that was it. She was never really a topic of discussion because he was turning into my new man.

Our relationship probably lasted for a year, but throughout that year, I faced many battles. There were constant arguments, fights, and other women. The bad outweighed the good the entire time we were together. A few years after the breakup, my cousin started dating him and got pregnant, but she had an abortion. A few years later, a friend of mine had his 6th or 7th child. But honestly, I could name a few more people I was cool with, but I'm hoping you get the point.

Even though I got the relationship I wanted at the time, but I eventually got out. I STILL DIDN'T WIN. In my mind I believed when I first got him, I had won. Like I had to prove a point. Only to realize I had gained absolutely nothing during our time together except heartache and pain. Making a decision based on lustful desire, came back to haunt me, time and time again. Because I acted based on a lustful desire and a malicious motive, came back and bite me in the ass.

As the years passed by, I realized that to him I was just another girl willing to give up my body, especially after he messed with a lot of my friends. But to blame him and not blame myself would be crazy. Even though I notice him before I seem him with Michelle, my motive changed once I did.

Yes, I still wanted him but a part of me wanted to show her that she doesn't run anything. Her attitude, the way she talked, walked, and acted rubbed me wrong I felt I had too. Only for my motive for her to come back to haunt me from someone else. Different people different places. Karma doesn't have a certain time that she will come back around. When you are doing something, you have no business doing, it's coming back. You can't run from it and you can't hide. I acted based on a lustful desire soon turning into a malicious motive. Getting nothing out of it except; abuse, hurt, and pain.

Never allow that lustful desire to have control over you. When you don't have total control of that desire, you allow yourself and the object of your desire to experience a lot of things that were never meant to be. Even if the person you desire encourages your feelings, don't allow yourself to play the game he or she is playing. It says a lot about your character and who you are. Others may never know what you have done behind closed doors, but God does and that's enough in itself.

2.4: You Want to Be Grown

It was two months after my seventeenth birthday, and I was sitting in a small room at Palmetto Pregnancy Center. Afraid. I was patiently waiting on the counselor to return with the test result. I had already taken one at home which was positive, but I needed the center to confirm for me. All kinds of thoughts were racing through my head but the thought of becoming a mother was a bit overwhelming.

There was a slight tap at the door, "May I come in?" The counselor asked as she walked into the room. Walking to sit down beside me, "Well Ms. Strong, your test did come back positive. You are pregnant." Glancing at the floor, my eyes started to water so fast that tears begin to fall. I wasn't ready to be called mommy when I was still saying it myself. I wasn't ready to grow up and handle mother responsibilities the way my mother was. I was only a junior in high school. I wasn't ready to give up band, partying all the time with my friends, and it been all about Marti'ka. I just wasn't ready.

"Are you ok Marti'ka? Babies are a blessing so don't cry but you do have options that are available to you!" The counselor was now trying to cheer me up. "Yes ma'am! I guess. This is a hard pill to swallow. I just turned 17 and I'm only a junior in high school. How am I going to tell my momma?" I asked the counselor with concerned eyes. Reaching to grab my hand, "Ms. Strong, everything will be okay. Let us do an ultrasound to see how far along you are and I will explain the options available to you." The counselor tried to make eye contact with me, but I found myself glancing at the monitor and bed that was sitting in the room. I now hated that I was all alone, and I wish I wasn't.

"Okay, that's fine!" I told the counselor as she was directing me to get onto the table. I hesitated at first, but I slowly put my purse in the chair I was sitting in, so I could lay back on the table. Not only was I scared because I was alone, but I also wasn't sure who the father was. It was only between two people. One dude that I had been sleeping with for two years and another dude I had started dating two months prior to my confirmation.

"Now Ms. Strong, I need you to just relax. Can you unbutton your pants please?" she asked as she was grabbing a tube. Reaching to unbutton my pants, I started feeling butterflies in my stomach. I wasn't sure if it was the flutter from the baby or me just being nervous. Maybe it was a combination but seeing a baby inside me was a moment that I wasn't ready for.

"Ms. Strong, I'm going to apply some gel onto your stomach, and it will be cold. Just take a deep breath if you need too" she said. Closing my eyes to prepare myself to see the baby, I answered ok and took a deep breath. "Next, I will be taking the probe to spread the gel across your stomach. Once I start spreading the gel out, you will be able to see your little one." The counselor was talking with more excitement in her voice then I had in my heart.

Opening my eyes, all I seen was a little body moving inside me. At that very moment, the only thing I could do was stare. I knew then that the only option that was available to me was for me to become a mother. It was now time to face reality.

Watching as she sizes the baby and check for my estimated due date. Wondering how I was going to break this news to my mother and both possibilities. "Ms. Strong you are almost 8 weeks pregnant, and your estimated due date is September 19." She said as she hit the print button on the screen to print copies of the ultrasound. Handing me a paper towel so I could wipe my stomach off. "You can have a seat back in the chair you were sitting in if you like." Encouraging me to get comfortable so we could discuss my options. I buckled up my pants, threw the paper towel away and moved back to the chair I placed my purse in.

"So, Ms. Strong you do have three different options to choose from. You can become a mother or have the baby and choose adoption. Lastly, we don't support this option here at Palmetto Pregnancy Center, but you could abort if you chose." Hearing my choices, I screamed "NO! I know what I want to do. I'm going to keep the baby."

"Great!" with more excitement in the counselor's voice, she handled me a package for mothers-to-be. "In this package!" She was now trying to explain to me what was in the package. I no longer wanted to hear what she was saying - I was ready to go. I needed to call my best-friend to let her know that we were about to have a baby on the way. She was the only one I wanted to talk to at the current moment before I broke the news to anyone else.

I was only 17 for two months before I was hit with the baby fever. I could no longer ponder on the past, but it was now time to embrace my new journey as a mother. My life was changed forever. The only choice now was to prepare both of us for greatness.

2.5: Children Out Of Wedlock:

Teenage Motherhood

Thirteen years ago, I never thought I would become a teenage mother, much less a single mother. 28% of households have only one parent raising children in America and I never thought I would be part of that count.

It was a hard transition for me, coming and going I was used to getting everything, come and go as I please, and didn't have any responsibilities. I really was still a baby and legally I wasn't even considered an adult.

After having my son, all the things I was used to having and doing changed. I moved out my mother house so I could learn how to live without her. I needed to know how to work, pay bills, and take care of my household just in case something happened to my mother. I didn't know how to do anything except go to school, work, keep the house clean, and cook small things. In my eyes, I was an adult now and it was time to grow up. It was now time to take on life and the responsibilities that come with it.

I love my children very much. Despite all the things I have been through, I just look up to the sky and say THANK YOU JESUS for everything. Over the last thirteen years of my life, I have faced the many ups and downs of being a single mother. I learned to balance my own apartment, graduate college, and working, all the while raising two kids. Although I have managed to accomplish a lot, my life has not been easy.

When my first child was two years old, I was working at a Wal-Mart in the next city, about 15 minutes from my house, for nine hours each day at night. I took classes at my town's college for nearly four hours in the morning. On top of that, I also had a work-study job at school.

My life was constantly on go. While I reasoned that I wanted to go to college locally to be near my baby, I was still living a life that didn't really include my child. I didn't know what it really meant to be a mother because I was too busy trying to chase my dreams, grow up, and have a ball. It took a while before I finally grew to acknowledge that I couldn't live a normal, busy 19-year-old life that focused on my wants. I had a two-year-old son.

So, I encourage everyone not to be in a rush to grow up. Don't be eager to have sex because you feel like not having it is boring. Don't allow this world to fool you and trap you in sin and becoming a young teenage parent. Focus on what really matters. Trying to chase a dream and been a young single mother can send you in all kinds of directions you never anticipated. You have less time and energy for yourself, which makes reaching that dream far more complicated.

My choice to become a young mother has been nothing but a blessing. As the years went by, I had to learned to adapt to my new life. I created a list of things that I needed to be a top priority in my life which I would love to share with you. From my experiences, I learned that I needed to center my life around these things to find personal success for my life. Let's start with the most important priority to me.

JESUS:

Now before I move forward, I'm not trying to force Jesus on anyone because you are entitled to believe what you want to. This is just from my personal experience.

I grew up in a Baptist church so praising the Lord was put in me since birth. I was taught the word, learned the word, and I always kept it in me no matter what I did. I hear a lot of people say that Jesus isn't real, and the bible is manmade. Yet, every time I have called on the name of Jesus, He has always came through.

I remember praying to God asking Him to bless me with a career that I would love. A place that I could go to everyday and love what I do. Watching my mother growing up, I didn't want to be that way. I didn't want to settle for anything just to provide for my boys. I wanted to love what I do, be able to come home to my boys at a decent time, cook for them and help with their homework. I wanted to make my baby football games and I wanted to take them places more than once a year. I wanted to do this for them while still elevating into the next season of my life without the struggle.

Attempt after attempt I was doing different things to make good money but none of those things made my heart smile until I was introduced to massage therapy in 2014. I am not where I want to be yet, but God has blessed me with a career that I love while making great money doing it. Since becoming a massage therapist in 2015, I have been out of town about 12 times, only work about 20 hours a week and my hours are the bomb. Most people can't say they love what they do or can't afford to constantly travel as they feel. So that is a blessing within itself.

Looking at my old list of goals to accomplish, massage therapy wasn't on there. It was something that God bought out of me that He put in me when I prayed for it. No matter what someone may say, I know where my help come from.

I know who the source of everything is and I know that I am covered by the blood of Jesus.

SELF-LOVE:

The journey of loving self sometimes can be the hardest journey that you could ever take. Loving self isn't always easy especially if the people close to you doesn't make you feel love.

I know what it is like to fight the battle of self-love. Settling for whatever just to feel love. I allowed the vision of who I am to fade away because I surrounded myself around people that constantly hurt me. Different people, different situation but the same result. Hurt. I learned something from each situation, but it took a lot from me. I had become broken. I had become lost. I didn't have enough fight to properly love my babies because I didn't know how to love myself. There were times I didn't even have any fight. I didn't want the hand that had been dealt to me. I wanted to throw it in the trash. Get rid of it.

I had to stop and investigate myself. I went back to that little girl in my room and reflect on the vision that God gave me at a young age. I had to move out my way, so God could lead. I had to become the woman that He was calling me to be.

It has been a process and I haven't always gotten it right, but after so many heart aches, failures, disappointments, and lack of self, it was time for a change. It didn't happen overnight, and I am and will forever be a working progress.

The most important thing I have learned about self-love is no one can love you like you can love you. There is no love in someone else if you can't find it in yourself first.

Sometimes you must let go of everything and everyone to find out who you really are. I encourage you not to let another day go by without learning something new about yourself. Whether you like it or not, learn who you are and if there is something that needs to be corrected, fix it.

Save yourself the hurt by learning who you truly are so you can become who you are called to be. No one can help you with self-love. That is between you and God.

EDUCATION:

Education is powerful but only when it's applied wisely and used correctly. Having a great education goes beyond high school. Education requires teaching and educating yourself daily. Allowing self to grow and elevate in different areas outside of the norm.

Knowledge is something that no one can take away from you. People can strip you of everything you have, but they can't take your mind unless you let them. Don't allow anybody to play tricks, games, or control you because you refused to learn the things you needed to know in life. Educate yourself as much as possible to make decisions wisely. For example, when I was signing up for college, I educated myself on my major, the school, and the classes required to graduate. When it was time to register, I was able to inform my guidance counselor of the classes I wanted to take each semester based off what I knew I could handle for each semester. I didn't allow him to choose my classes and I was fully aware of my classes taken. I took ownership in making sure I complete the program by being on top of everything.

Now I'm not saying that people can't help, educate, or guide you but it is best to always try to be ahead of the game by educating yourself on whatever you trying to accomplish.

FAMILY:

Family is important! Family should be your support system, the ones who push you into the next level of life! The ones who should correct you when you wrong and happy for you when you are succeeding.

Now I know the saying "blood is thicker than water" is so true. However, everyone that you call family is not always related by blood. You can have spiritual family, a best friend, a childhood friend, or someone you got close to in a short amount of time who brings out your best. Family encourages you to live your best life to your full potential. They will encourage you, lift you up, and love on you unconditional, but real family will also correct you when you are wrong.

For example, I was dating this guy that wasn't really on my level. He didn't bring anything to the table and honestly, he took more than he gave. Emotionally, physically, financially, and spiritually, I always gave more.

I finally decided to leave that situation and soon got into a relationship that wasn't much better. My sister would always tell me "Marti'ka I wish you find someone that will love you for you and stop settling with anybody just to say you have someone."

At the time, I heard her but there were a lot of factors that contributed to me settling, like sex – it was my drug and the fear of being alone. I wasn't the type to have sex with multiple man at the same time so I would find one that I thought I loved and settled for that. Being that she is my sister, there was a constant conversation that never ended.

It wasn't like she was telling me something wrong. She was telling me to love myself enough to stop settling for anybody just to please my flesh or deal with my fears.

There are some people in our lives that are family that we must walk away from, but family is what and who help mode you into the person God is calling you to be. I encourage you to love and cherish your family because once they are gone, you can't get them back.

Not everything they do and say is to harm you because some of the things said may really hold some truth to it. So, take what you need and spit the rest out. Family is not all that bad.

Becoming a teenage mother hasn't been easy but along the road of being one, I had to learn the importance of those things listed above. Yes, it has been helpful for me, but it will also help to mode my boys into the men they are called to be. So, I encourage you daily, build your relationship with God, love who He has created you to be, educate yourself about everything, and allow family to push you through.

2.6: Why The Health Department Calling Me?

It was a long day at school and all I wanted was to go home and relax before work. I had just walked into my room, sat on my bed, to take my shoes off. Speaking to my sister but nothing major, I slowly started to drift off into my own world when my phone begun to ring. Looking at the phone, I notice the number. Only because it was the same number that I called to schedule my appointment for an annual physical.

Answering the phone, "Hello." with a crack in my voice. "Yes, may I speak with Marti'ka Strong please?" The lady asked on the other end. "This is she. How may I help you?" I asked with an attitude, wondering why. "My name is Lisa Long, and I am calling from the Health Department. Your test results have come back, and you tested positive for chlamydia." She paused briefly before she continued. "Now this is a curable STD, so I need you to come back in and it only requires one dosage." I wanted to put the phone down because I didn't want to hear what she was saying. My sister was now staring with a nasty look on her face.

"Ms. Strong." The lady was now calling my name. "Yes ma'am? I'm so sorry. I just lost focus for a second." I said. I really wasn't sure how many times she called my name.

"When can you come in Ms. Strong? We close today at 5pm if you can come before then." My current situation had me lost for word. I was just going to the health department to get an annual checkup. I wasn't expecting a positive STD report. "I can come over now before I head to work. I'm on my way. Be there in about 15 minutes." She thanked me and said to ask for her when I got there.

Not wanting to look at my sister, she asked what was all that about before I could even get a word out. I let her know I tested positive for chlamydia as I sat back down on my bed in shame. "Ugh, that's nasty." She said as she turned to focus on whatever she was doing before. Adding more fire to the flame, I changed my clothes for work and walked out the door.

Unsure of what chlamydia really was, I knew where it came from. I was talking to this dude at Clinton College, and we had sex once. For some reason when we first started, he didn't wear any protection but 5 minutes in, he decided to put one on. Silly me, I should have told him to wear one from the beginning, but I allowed myself to get caught up in the moment. I cried my entire ride there.

Pulling up at the health department, I hurried inside so I could get the process started and over with. I couldn't believe that I haven't had sex with five people yet and I was experiencing "You are positive" bug. I didn't know how to feel, and I was afraid to talk to anyone about it. I grabbed my medicine, took the pills, and headed to work, attempting to be happy and make it through the rest of the day. I knew that my life would be different, and I would never look at myself the same again.

2.7: You Tested Positive

Did your eyes get big when you read the topic for this section? Well, mine did when I heard my test results was positive for chlamydia over the phone. When you have sex before marriage, this result is possible. It's nothing to play with, but many people are just having sex without realizing the dangers at hand.

Not only are you at risk of physical STDs, but you are also at risk spiritually as well. Sex is supposed to occur between a husband and a wife - not just with Ben, Sam, and Trey. The only way God honors sex is when you are married, man and woman.

If I could go back to the age of 13 when I lost my virginity, I would have left that boy where he was at. I didn't realize the door I was opening in my life, allowing all different kind of spirits to attach to me. I also learned along the way that whenever you have sex with someone who is or was promiscuous, spiritually you are having sex with all those other people, too. You have now opened the door to spirits those people is battling with. For example, if you had sex with 1 person but that person has had sex with 15 people. You become spiritually involved with 16 people instead of one. Even if there is protection against physical STDs, there is no shield against spiritual diseases.

Everyone has a story to tell, and luckily some don't include having a STD. However, mine does. I am just thankful that it has never been life-threatening. If you have a story that includes an STD in your past or present, I encourage you to tell your story. It might just save a life or two. I encourage everyone to cross their legs and wait on God to send your ordained spouse. But if you feel that you haven't reached that point yet, then make sure that you protect yourself. One time can change your lifetime.

2:8: Loneliness: Why Do I Feel So Alone

During some point in life, loneliness will try and find a way to enter your life. Whether it is by choice or force, it something that I believe everyone will face one day. Even when I was surrounded around family, friends, co-workers, etc., that loved me, I still felt alone.

I have learned there are certain seasons in life where God will put you in the wilderness to elevate you. However, other times you can put yourself there. I traveled the path of loneliness because I felt like I needed a man all the time and sex were one of the ways to keep him. I felt that I had to be connected to a guy and I had to be sexually attracted to him as well.

Every time I ended a relationship, I turned around and got into another one. I never allowed myself the time to heal and learn who I truly was. I battled with the feeling of loneliness for years because I was constantly looking for a man to fill the emptiness in my heart. I did not search for God's love, and I felt like no one really loved me.

As I mentioned earlier, my battle with loneliness first began because my father left. I blamed him for not being there. I blamed him for not teaching me how to love myself and not to allow men to use me. I blamed him for my choices that I made because I had a void missing in my life. A void that I tried to fill with sex, so I wouldn't have to deal with my loneliness. Attempting to fill the void on my own, I caused myself a lot of heartache and pain.

To overcome loneliness, I first had to learn to forgive my father, seek God for answers and love, and grow up. You can't blame people for your choices once you reach a certain age in life. I remember two sayings while growing up: "Age ain't nothing but a number" and "The age doesn't determine your maturity." These sayings are true, but they overlook the fact that, once you reach about 12, you start becoming responsible for your soul. Legally when you are 18, your parents no longer have to provide for you.

You must grow up one day and let go of your past. Those hurts of your past must be forgiving. The sooner you decide to forgive your past, the sooner your personal growth can begin.

So, my question to you is: Have you ever experienced loneliness in your life that is caused you to search for love in all the wrong places? Allowing yourself to settle for less just so you won't feel alone? You believe that your soul is prospering but you never stop to look and realize you are dying in the inside? Leaving you empty inside settling for love.

Loneliness is painful to experience, and it is easy to use that blinding pain to make excuses. Have you ever been so lonely that you felt like the entire world was against you? No one else could give you any advice because you believed they didn't really care. Maybe you had sex with multiple men, and now you don't feel worthy anymore. Or maybe you are single with children, and because of them, you believe no one will marry you? So, you blame other people for feeling alone. You refuse to look at your own actions or accept any truth because you don't want to hear about your loneliness. Better yet, you don't want to accept it.

Excuses only add to the problem instead of helping to fix it. The more you fight with the "whys" of everything in your life that made you feel the way you do, the more you will continue to fight with loneliness.

Loneliness is possible to accept without regrets. First, you must learn as a person what may trigger the feelings of loneliness. Then, when you face those triggers, remember you are never alone when you have a Father by the name of Jehovah and a friend, a brother, and a savior named Jesus. To find these triggers, reflect over your life and think about all the bad times and events that God has bought you out of safely. Look at those times where only God's aid could have saved you. You have never been alone, even when you didn't acknowledge God in your life.

So, let's look at some triggering factors; they can be events in the past, people in the present, or old, bad relationships. Write down at least the top three things that have caused you a lot of pain in life that you have not yet let go of.

1._____

2._____

3._____

Now explain why these things hurt you or made you mad. How long have you held on to the hurt, and why are you still holding on to it?

1._____

2._____

3._____

I battled with the spirit of loneliness for years, blaming my father for his absence and looking for love in all the wrong places. But the more I did these things, the more I saw myself as worth less than what I am to God. I opened the door because, instead of holding onto the Word of God, I held onto childhood pain. Psalm 27:10 "When my father and my mother forsake me, then the LORD will take me up."

When you are made whole in Christ Jesus, there is no such thing as loneliness. Your relationship with God should be so intimate that nothing else even matters. Once you focus on God as your husband and yourself as His bride, God will give you your ordained husband. Now I know this is easier said than done, but trust in what I am telling you and give it ALL to Jesus. Below I listed a few scriptures that may encourage you if you are dealing with loneliness.

Deuteronomy 31:6 "Be strong and of a good courage, fear not, nor be afraid of them: for the LORD thy God, he *it is* that doth go with thee; he will not fail thee, nor forsake thee." (KJV)

1 Peter 5:7 "Casting all your care upon him; for he careth for you." (KJV)

Psalm 147:3 "He healeth the broken in heart, and bindeth up their wounds." (KJV)

Know that when you are feeling alone and need someone to talk to, Jesus is right there. He is a true friend indeed. You are never alone.

2.9: You Not Ready

"Will you marry me?" My boyfriend asked me as he got down on one knee with the ring in his hand. The ring was sitting pretty in a nice small black box.

"No! You are not ready for marriage." I said to him as I started to walk away. "I haven't seen you since 6 o'clock yesterday and you were supposed to be coming to the house right after me. What type of proposal is this?" Even though I did love him, but I knew I couldn't set myself up. We dated for about 2½ years and the ride was most definitely a roller coaster.

About a year in, I found out he had a girlfriend, which he was going back and forward between us. I allowed myself to keep dealing with him because I was in love with him. I wanted him to decide between her or me. Either way, I was becoming drained from all the mess that came with him.

About 6 months later, he told me that he wanted to be with me and me only. He packed his things and moved in with me. We lived together for a month before he decided to propose to me. He wasn't working, had / kids, and was still playing games. I needed to see some growth in him. I needed to see a change before I could take that vow to say, "I do!"

"What you mean I am not ready? I am ready! You must not be ready!" He said as he started walking behind me. It was an early Sunday morning in March when this occurred, but how could he be ready to become my husband when he just lied to my face on yesterday. We were having a cookout at my cousin house and by the time he arrived, it was time to go. He had gotten up early that morning and left the house. Something was wrong with his phone, so I couldn't call him. For some reason, it wouldn't keep a charge to it.

We had both agreed we were heading home to relax and enjoy the rest of the night. Well, he never made it home till the next morning. Walking into the house, he gave me a sorry excuse as to why he didn't come home last night. Only to get on one knee to propose right afterward.

I felt played in so many ways. He knew my past and my desire to one day be married. I even took him back a few times after all the back and forward mess with the other women. He must have thought I was weak. He thought he had my mind gone, that I was going to say "Yes." Ha! Well not today I was not. My answer was no, and I meant just that.

Our relationship only lasted till September of that same year before I decided to call it quit. We broke up like one more time before I was officially done with the games and the lies. I wanted to be left alone and single. I just wanted to enjoy me and my boys. I deserved to be happy and loved the correct way and he made it clear to me that he could not do it.

****

From September to December, he would call me every day wanting to talk and work things out. But I could not do. I blocked his calls and on Facebook to prevent any forms of contact from him. That still did not stop him from calling me. He would still leave songs and messages on my voicemails, hoping that I would give in.

It was on Christmas Eve when I decided to change my number. I had the same number for almost 10 years. I only had 1 one day left before I hit my 10-year anniversary. My first cell phone number I had to say goodbye to it because the messages would not stop. I did not want to change it, everyone knew that number, but I was tired of the messages.

The next day, I was scrolling down my Facebook page when I seem his nephew post a picture of him and some woman getting married. *Wait!* I thought as my eyes started to tear up, *who is this woman? How could he marry her within the same year of asking me to marry him? It had only been 3 months since we had broken up. It was too soon for him to be marrying someone else.*

I know I had told him no! I know that I blocked him and every time he would pop up at my house, my mother's house, and even my cousin's, I told him no. I didn't tell him no because I didn't love him. I told him no because I wanted him to get himself together. My no did not mean go marry someone else 3 months after we broke up. My Christmas was ruined. And to make matters worse, it wasn't even the other woman I had been going back and forward with about him. She was someone I didn't know and I had never seen her face before.

Who was this woman that stole his heart from me? There were some many questions that I wanted to ask him, but I couldn't. I couldn't because I no longer had that right. I told him no. I blocked him from calling or texting me. I even changed my number so he could never call me again. I was hurting and I soon became angry that I told him no.

I ran into him on Valentine's Day. He wanted to talk, so we decided to meet at the park and talk. I needed closure because I was hurting. We talked and I was able to ask him why he married her? How could he do me like that? His response was, "You told me that I was not ready to get marry. I told you I was ready, but you told me no." Sitting in the passenger seat of his car listening to him talk as tears fell down from my face. I felt like I had missed my opportunity to become a Mrs. Wiping my tears, he told me that he had something for me later that day and to meet him back at the park in a few hours.

Hours passed as I was waiting on him to call me to meet him at the park. Waiting patiently, my feelings were all over the place and the emotional rollercoaster he had taken me on during our relationship, made me feel like I was back on it. But this time, I knew I had to get off it for good because by law and in God's eyes he now belonged to someone else. Sitting in a daze, my phone rings and it was him telling me to meet him back at the same park from earlier. "Ok!" I said, rushing to see what he had for me. Knowing that it wasn't right to receive anything from him, but my last 2 Valentine's Day were with him, so I felt I deserved something from all the hell he had previously taken me through.

Arriving at the park, he was sitting in the parking lot waiting on me. I got out my car and got into his. He handed me a card and flowers. Opening the card, it was $50 in there and written on the card Happy Valentine's Day. The gift bought more tears to my eyes. I was thankful for the gift but hurt at the same time. He gave me a hug and before I got out the car, I told him, "I am glad that I didn't marry you because if the shoe was on the other foot, I would be pissed if you were giving your ex something for Valentine's Day." Even though she probably did not but I knew what was going on and I honestly did not like it. I got out the car and told him thank you.

Healing from this experience was hard to do because I always desired to get married. I was ready to be someone wife. I wanted that love that would last forever. I had fell in love with someone that did not love me the same way. Through it all the most important thing I learned from the situation was, don't settle no matter how much it hurts to walk away. He offered to give me something I wanted, marriage. But he also shown me after he married someone else, that marriage with him wasn't what was best for me. It took some time to heal from it, but I am thankful today that I told him no. The pain at the moment did not feel good but I do believe that my no protected me from more hurt and pain in the long run. Never regret your no. Stand on it and be ok with waiting on the right one for marriage.

2.10: Don't Write A Check You Can't Cash

I don't know about you, but I have put myself in situation where I have written a check that I couldn't cash. To be real, I have written plenty of them. Regardless, if I could cash it or not, I wrote it. Not even thinking about the consequence behind it, which is the wrong mentality to have.

I'm not the type of person to brag or talk about the things I do. Whether I am doing it for someone else or just accomplishing something in life, it is not for everyone to know. But there was a check I wrote that would soon return.

I decided to help this young lady out that I had been knowing for about 3 years. I did not know her on a personal level at first, but we stayed in the same neighborhood so over time I got to know her better. One day she made a post about walking her babies to school in the cold. It was about a 10 minutes' drive from her house to the school, so on foot was a walk.

I did not want that for her babies so I reached out to her and told her on the days I didn't have to work, I would come take them to school. Over a 6-month period of helping, I didn't ask for anything. No gas or even an effort to give when she did have.

I didn't ask because as I was taking her babies to school, we started building a bond with each other. She started opening up and telling me some of the things she had been through. I eventually became that friend that wanted to show her that someone did love her, and she could do whatever she set her mind to do. She wasn't alone and some of her pains were my pains as well.

As I got closer to her, I started taking her kids to school every day, feeding them, giving her everyday items that she needed and that is only to name a few. Whatever she needed; I was there. Just trying to be a friend and help but I soon found out that someone else's problem should never become mine.

I quickly realized I had dedicated my life to her every day by helping in some type of way. I felt like she needed a hand, and I knew I couldn't do much, but there were small things I could help with. I didn't mind because my boys and I are truly blessed.

Over the 6-month period she stayed at four different places and one stop was my house before I had to cut all ties. I felt like she needed love. After listening to her talk about how no one loves her and everyone uses her, I wanted to show her someone does care. I knew about some of her situation growing up and I seem a lot of things in her that I battled with before. She is a very beautiful and smart girl. I loved her and her three children like she was my little sister, and they were my niece and nephews. Whatever I could do, I did without a problem. Still smiling and helping through my own rain.

We were together all the time and talked every day so when she got put out, I opened my big mouth. I opened my house to her and her kids, something I told myself I would never do. I had seemed a lot of bad results from letting other people move in your house. I didn't even realize I had now written a check that would soon bounce back in sevens day and I wasn't prepared for the result.

I open my home with only a few rules:

1. Purchase own washing powder and deodorant!

2. Have the kids fed, bathed, and in the bed no later than 9:30 p.m.
3. Help with keeping the house clean.

I only worked two night in which I would be home by 9 p.m. On those nights, all she had to do was feed the kids and get them ready for bed. (My boys can give themselves baths and get their night clothes, so technically she was only giving her kids bath).

Unfortunately, my three rules must have been too much to handle because she only gave her kids a bath 1 nights. Only because she was trying to go somewhere, and I told her she need to give her kids a bath. The first and second night I came home from work, the kids had not eaten- even though it was already cooked. All she had to do was warm up the food which she refused to do, and no one had their baths.

Instead, she washed clothes that day and relaxed the rest of the day as if there was nothing that needed to be done. She was waiting on me to do it. She also refused to purchase her own detergent, stating she didn't have any money, but she had money to buy a box of cigarette and junk from Wal-Mart the day before.

She had gotten so comfortable with me helping her that when it was time to step up to the plate, she wouldn't do it. She wanted me to do it. She didn't care about me working, cooking, and running her around while still handling my duties. She wanted what she wanted and used me to get it because I was trying to be a friend looking out for someone in need.

I walked into a battle that wasn't mine to fight. She used the excuse that because her mother wasn't there, she didn't know how to be a mother. She was waiting on me to do it, which I did until I realized I was now taking care of 6 people and I was truly neglecting my kids. I was neglecting myself because I was now stressing and aggravated all the time because I was trying to constantly help someone else out.

I realized I was the one being played. I was being used for the things she could get and if she needed to keep doing that, it was okay with her. I loved her but I had to put my foot down. They had to go. So, I sat her down and told her how I felt. Only for her to moved next door to my neighbor and start a lot of mess because she didn't want to truly accept responsibility that she needed too.

She threw a rock and tried to hide her hand but through it all, I learned that you must be careful of the check you chose to write. Some checks just aren't worth cashing better yet writing.

When I look back over the situation, it caused more pain to me, but it made me look at myself. Not to judge anyone, but I had to ask myself how I always end up in situation where I am constantly giving and not receiving. How is this happening in both relationship with females and males. I wanted to know why I was so vulnerable and just couldn't accept people for who they are when they first show me.

I needed to find the good in other people because I felt like if people would take the time to get to know me, they would truly see my heart. Overall, I know that change only comes from the willingness to try. If you never try you will remind stuck like a tree instead of soaring like an eagle. So instead of trying to write a check that you know might bounce, find a different route. A route that will cause you less trouble in the end.

(Word of Advice: Always listen to your first instinct. Your gut be trying to warn you).

2.11: Never Make A Friend Because You Lonely

I battled over and over with adding this to the book, but I realized that this was a battle that I had to defeat, jump over, and conquer. Mentioned previously before, I battle with loneliness and I feared being alone. My past had me running to people that I called my friends. People that I though dealt with me the same way I dealt with them until reality hit me. Those people were never, ever my friends.

When I was battling with loneliness, not only did I attach myself to the wrong guys but also the wrong females. It seems like every female that I got close with betrayed me in way. I did not really understand why because I was not a disloyal person. I was real to my friends. Even though I may have shown my friendship differently from others, I was not the type of person to stab you in the back. If I call you friend that was one thing you will never have to worry about.

I remember in high school becoming friend with this girl that knew my child's father (my boyfriend at the time), was talking too and having sex with someone else. At the time this event was going on, me and the girl had not been friend maybe no more than a year. I found out she knew when everything started coming out. I never said anything to her about it.

I kept my feelings about the situation to myself. I felt a certain way because she knew and never told me until I bought the situation to her attention. I felt betrayed to a certain extent.

Over the years our friendship was on and off. There were seasons when we talked all the time and then there were seasons, we did not talk at all. But every friend or person has a reason for being in your life.

During the last three years of our friendship, we went to Myrtle Beach for Memorial Weekend. Going just to have fun, whether we had a room or not. A lot of money or not, we were there. Me and her like two peas in a pot. We were on go.

The last time we went, we met up with this guy, whom I was in love with and his homeboy. Even though we weren't in a relationship, he had a piece of my heart for a few years. He gave me butterflies being in his presence and I wouldn't know what to say. I was always nervous for some strange reason.

While at the beach, she hooked up with his homeboy and he was mine. Well at least at the time, I thought he was. Instantly, she exchanged numbers with him, soon calling him best friend. They started talking to each other on a regular basis and chilling together. She would tell me that he would ask about me, but she would tell him to leave me alone because he wasn't serious. The whole time my senses were saying otherwise. It got to the point where she started deciding when I could see, talk, or be alone with him. The ball was no longer in my court, but that is if it ever really was.

I voiced my opinion about their relationship but neither one of them cared about my feelings. What they had going on was way more important than little old me. My feelings didn't matter so I eventually moved out the way and let them do whatever.

There was time I couldn't sleep thinking about the betrayal. I wanted to cruse them out for hurting my feelings, but I realized it was pointless. I prayed about it and gave it to God. I wanted to reach out, but I couldn't. I had to be patience and allow the entire situation to play out.

After two years of wondering if my feelings were correct about them, out of the blue, she texted me telling me that he wanted to be with her. Some of the things she said in the text were the same thing she told me a few months before but this time the words were changed around. It was confirmation for me. My feelings were right. I knew it was more to what she said. She never told me everything, but it was no need too. Telling me that he wanted to be with her told me enough.

Reading that text that morning took something out of me. It hurted to know one of my closest friends that I genuinely cared for had crossed me out the equation and started her own thing with him. It broke me, but it made me stronger because I have always said "God remove those that don't mean me no good." And that is exactly what He did. Removed them completely so I would not go back.

After sitting back and evaluating our friendship, I realized something – even though I loved her, we had nothing in common. We were on different journeys in life and always have. I realized that when people show you who they are the first time, believe them. I should have known if she didn't care to tell me that my boyfriend at the time was cheating on me with her friend back in high school, she wasn't really my friend then.

I tried to make something out of a friendship that was never supposed to have started. Listen to the red flags with friendship as well. Those signs could help prevent a lot of disloyal people in your life.

2.12: Bad Habits Can Corrupt Your Character

Have you ever been in a situation where you said that you would never do something? You look at it or people with disgust because you feel you are better than them or it? "I would never do that," you tell yourself but find yourself doing the exact same thing you said you would never do.

Oh man! I have done it so many times and honestly, I probably will do it again if I am alive. I stand to say before I got pregnant with my oldest baby, I would look at people with disgust because they were smoking weed. I couldn't understand why they were doing it. To me they looked stupid, and I didn't like it.

Then senior week, a time when high school graduates from all over the southeast go to Myrtle Beach to celebrate, my life changed forever. I left my small city as a clear head young teenage mother needing to find myself again. Not thinking about smoking weed and most definitely not turning into a weed head. I was free at that moment. Free from responsibilities. Free from being a mother. Free from the new me.

On the way to the beach, I was the designated driver for my homeboys, and my cousin and friends were following behind us. Two people in the car were smokers. They smoked the entire way, rolling up blunts back-to-back, which caused me to get high from being closed in.

My cousin and one of my friends were also smokers. They had their own weed and the guys had theirs. Once we got checked in and settled into the room, the smoking session begun. I smoked the entire trip and, returned home to a newborn baby, searching for weed. I became a weed head very quickly. I was now using weed to deal with my stress, and it was now my way out.

For years I smoked to deal with the fact I was a young single mother, I didn't have anyone I really trust, and my dreams of going off to college were over. Everything that I planned for my life was ruined and no matter what I may have done to replace some of the things I could no longer do, it just wasn't the same.

I was still able to go to college, but I stayed in Rock Hill. I had my own place, but it was housing authority. I went from no government assistance to everything government assistance. I was only pregnant for 9 months, but I had a child forever. I couldn't go as I pleased and there were plenty times, I no longer could afford to do a lot of things that I use to do.

My life had taken a sharp turn and I was not ready for the change. I was still hurting from my past and raising a child was not part of the plan. I needed to heal. I needed to let go but facing it caused to much pain. I smoked the pain away instead, thinking it was helping the situation, but it wasn't. The pain wasn't going away, and my habit wasn't either.

My battle with weed first started with trying to cover up my hurt. Not wanting nor willing to deal with it. Over the years, I realized that I couldn't smoke weed to hide from my pain. I had to deal with it. I had to learn to forgive the ones that hurt me and accept my journey for what it was.

I realized after fighting against others but mainly myself for years, that I had to deal with my pain no matter what. God had shown me a promising future and I knew that in order to get there, letting go, moving on, and loving me no matter what would help to push me there. Letting go of past hurt, moving towards my finish line, and loving people even when they know not what they do.

Even though weed had become my drug, I realized that my drug was really my pain. Only because I didn't want to deal with it. The weed was helping me cope for a moment but once the high was gone, the pain was still there.

It does not matter what drugs you take. The pain does not go away, in fact, it only gets worst. I encourage you instead of running to drugs to cope with it, just deal with it. Face it and conquer it. I promise that you will feel better in the end.

It is always the storm that you fight the longest and meant to destroy you, that will become the storm that pushes you into your destiny. Never allow someone to belittle you if you are going through a storm, instead you keep fighting to stand. Fight to make a change and become a better you.

Every tear I have cried will produce some fruit!

----Marti'ka Strong

Section Three:

Mental Battle. Silent Tears.

My mind is STRONG. No way will I lose this battle.

3.1: Battlefield Of The Mind

"Martika you think you know everything!"

"You are not my momma!"

"Why you have to be so judgmental about everything?"

"Oh boys! Here she goes."

"Y'all know she holy!"

"Leave me alone Martika!"

    These were the words I would sometimes hear from people that called me their friend. I didn't understand why every time I said something, I was considered being judgmental or trying to be someone mother? Or why I had to be called "holy" just because I have a relationship with God.

    Now to say my delivery was the best would be a lie, but to judge someone wasn't my thing. I am not the type to judge, but I am the type to ask questions. Not to say I'm better than anyone, but I have always been the type to try and make people think. I knew what my future held for me. I knew that whatever I was facing at the time it was temporary. That it wasn't going to last forever.

    If I told you, I loved you and hung around you, I was always challenging you to be better. "Chase your dreams" has always been my motto. I know I'm going to accomplish my goals and I wanted everyone around me to do the same. Yet hearing people say those things to me was like a battlefield of the mind. Each person is born with some type of gift and motivation is one of mine.

    The way they would respond to me made me feel like my gift was a bad thing. I only want to motivate but along that line of trying to motivate other people, the truth is required to be told. And honestly everyone doesn't want to hear the truth. I'm guilty of it myself. The truth hurt, but somewhere along the lines the truth gets water down. The truth will cut you so deep that living in that lie or denial feels better. Certain people will refuse the help sent to them to set them free.

    What was it about me that people assumed I knew it all? I have always asked a thousand questions and needed answer. Why the people I grew up with felt this way but people I just met would soak it up and receive it?

    It was a constant battlefield of my mind. One side was telling me I was wrong – I should agree with people, mind my business, and let them be. The other side was screaming, "You can't give up!" "You can't stop being you!" "It's people out there that need you!"

    Was it because these people seen my scars and thought I was still living there? They saw me in action when I didn't have a care in the world. When my mouth sometime spoke before I thought things through? Was I still been prosecuted for my past?

    On the other hand, people I didn't even grow up with love me for me. How could they see but the others couldn't?

I just needed answers. Is there something wrong with me or is it them that has the problem? Is it my boldness that scare them? Or their jealousy that offend them. Why is there something wrong with me encouraging them?

As I have battle with these questions for years, I come to the realization that it's not me. Its them. To say I'm perfect would be a lie but to say these other things about me are too. This battle. The battle of my mind. Sometimes I let them win without even showing it on the outside. Only because I wanted to know was it them or is it me?

People will hate you, dislike you, and even shoot down every word you say because they are mad. They are upset with their own lives. You can't except people to accept you when they don't even accept themselves. Be you and don't allow the battlefield of your mind to win.

3.2: Why You Mad?

Are you or have you ever been someone that looks at someone else's life and envy what they have? You sit there and compare yourself to them, trying to figure out a million ways to be better than them. A million things you could do to outdo them. Better yet, you won't even give credit to someone that actually deserves it. You may have said, "I am proud of you" knowing it wasn't the honest truth.

But why though? Why are you even mad? Did that person hurt you? Did they betray your trust? Did they do something so wrong to you and that's why you mad? Or to be honest with yourself you have no reason to be mad. You just see what they have and want it. You may not want to be them, but you don't want to be yourself either. They may have a house, nice car, chasing their career. They could be traveling, living their best life, and happy. Because you see it, you want it.

I will admit that I have done it before. For me, I wanted to hurry my process up. Not that I wanted exactly what someone else had, but more like being in a position that someone was in. I had to be honest with myself. I had to considered what someone may have been through. Especially knowing certain sacrifices, I had to make to get to where I am now.

Have you ever considered what that person may have went through to get to where they are and what they have? For instance, you want to buy a house. Have you taken the necessary steps to purchase? Maybe you want to start a successful business. Have you taken the time to write your vision out for your business? You want to be in love, but have you taken the time out to heal from before?

When someone accomplishes something in their life, they had to work for it. Whether it was accomplished in the right or wrong way, something was given in exchange. Never look at others and compare yourself. Why? Comparing yourself to others causes stagnation to occur in your life. If you are too busy looking at others, you forget to look at yourself.

You can have whatever you desire to have in life. It's up to you to go get it because no one is going to give you anything. Stop being mad or disliking someone that choses to live their life. You only have one life to live, and I suggest that you don't spend it on looking at what others got. Believe me, there is enough to go around for everyone!

3.3: The Unspoken Truth

The people you surround yourself with in life will either make you better or make you worse. They will teach you or dummy you down. They will help you or hinder you. They will love you or hate you. No matter what you do or who you are, their role will play a lesson in your life.

Over my lifetime of dealing with family and friends, I have learned that people will hold an unspoken truth about you. About how they really feel about you. These people will laugh with you but talk about you behind your back. They will judge you without evening providing a solution to the problem. They will look at you with hate in their eyes wishing to be you or to have traits like you. Not really knowing who they are, they will prosecute you. They will call you everything but who you really are.

Why? Because they see the reflection of who they really are and try to blame it on you. They aren't happy with themselves. Misery loves company!

So, I say to you, don't allow the way others feel about you to hinder you from being you. Learn how to live in your truth and be free. The unspoken truth that they will never say, will never be resolved because it doesn't exist in their eyes. Yet their actions can be felt, their words are different, and their motive isn't love.

Embrace yourself, love on you and most importantly love back on those that sincerely loves you.

3.4: Just Kill Yourself Already

"Don't nobody love you! I dare you to do it!" These were the thoughts running through my head. It was my 9th grade year in high school, and I found out that my boyfriend was cheating on me. We had gotten into a bad fight and I was really starting to feel depressed and unworthy. I was tired of feeling pain. I didn't want it anymore. I felt like no one loved me.

I didn't have a desire for life anymore and at the time I didn't think anyone would care if I just killed myself anyways. Sitting on the edge of the bed, my mother and stepfather was already in the bed sleep. I wasn't sure where my brother was, and my sister haven't arrived home just yet.

Looking at the pill bottle, I opened it with tears in my eyes. The bottle was full of naproxen, small blue pills for pain. Pouring a hand full, I put them into my mouth and swallowed. I was ready to end it all. Half of the bottle now gone, I attempted to pour the rest of the pills into my hand. At that same moment, my sister decided to walk into the door.

No lights were on in the house, only our room light. The way the house was built, you could see straight into our room from the living room. Looking into the room as she was walking by, she noticed the pills in my hand. "Momma, wake up! Momma!" She ran into our room screaming, as she slapped the pills out of my hand. "How many pills have you took. Asking me how many pills I had already taken.

"What? What's wrong?" My mother screamed back in panic mood rushing into our room. My sister was still talking to me trying to get me to respond. Looking at them with confusion, I wasn't trying to talk - I was only trying to die.

****

Arriving at the hospital, they rushed me to the back. I was questioned over and over by the doctor. Once he got all the information he needed, I was forced to drink charcoal. It was dark, thick, and nasty. It was designed to upset the stomach, to make me throw up everything on it. The number of pills I had taken, could have killed me. It was a must that it all came back up and out.

After throwing my stomach up and sitting in the emergency room for a while, I was finally released. I wasn't released to go home and act as if everything was normal. I was released to go home and ordered to seek professional counseling. To seek the correct help needed.

Attempting to commit suicide doesn't just come to mind over night. It comes from years of pain and thousands of unanswered questions. At least for me anyways. I was fighting a battle that started a long time ago in my life.

Either I wasn't ready to deal with the pain or I just didn't know how to. Regardless, I thought of ending my life was the answer. It wasn't my answer though because God kept me here for a reason. Trying to commit suicide doesn't solve the problem. Yes, it may seem like the best solution, but it isn't. It leaves love ones, family and friends in sorrow and regrets. If children are involved, they would be left without a parent.

Once I was able to get some healing and reflect on it, I believe it was a coward move to make. I wasn't thinking about anyone else but myself. I just didn't feel like dealing with the truth of my pain and being honest with myself. I preferred the easy route but instead God made me go through.

I encourage anyone that may have these types of thoughts, please seek some type of help. Find someone you can trust and talk to about whatever may be troubling you. You must talk about it and release it. Here are a few tips that may help you:

1. Please seek help
2. Learn to accept your pain
3. Find someone you can trust
4. Be honest with yourself
5. Forgive them. Forgiveness is for you
6. Don't be afraid or ashamed
7. Most importantly seek Jesus

I am thankful that God didn't allow it to happen. If He did, I wouldn't be here to tell my story. Remember that every testimony you have or will have, comes from a test!

3.5: Thank God For Your Judas

Have you ever had a person or even maybe a few people that you called friend? Y'all did everything together. From partying, taking some trips, and even going on double dates. Y'all shared some important and life changing experiences with each other. You knew this person would be your friend for life?

As much as you though that person was for you only to find out they aren't through an act of betrayal. They betrayed your trust. They went against the girl code. They did something they shouldn't have done and have you thinking like "Dang I didn't know it was like that with us!"

Well let me say this. I have been betrayed by a couple of people. Girls that I called friends went behind my back and told my business. Some even found a way to sleep behind my back with one of my past lovers.

You can have a circle of friends, thinking everyone is on the same page, not even realizing that there is a Judas floating around. Judas was the one who betrayed Jesus for silver. Judas is someone that you have in your close circle that is really praying for your downfall. They will trade in the friendship to fulfill a desire of their own.

Take a minute and evaluate the people you call friends. What is their character when it comes to you? Do they act different when others are around? Have y'all had any disagreements before? What was the causing factor of the disagreement? Could that person even admit to the part they may have played. Did they even apologize? Did they do it again?

As you think about your life and the friends you had growing up to now, how many of them fell off? How many are still holding on? Not all friendship ends from betrayal but for the ones that do. Leave them there. If someone has betrayed you before, what makes you think that they won't do it again?

When someone betrays you, instead of getting even, get glad. It is a hurtful feeling that no one ever wants to experience but God allowed it to happen. He allowed you to deal with it then so you would not have to deal with it later. Thank God that is one less thing to worry about along your journey to your finish line.

I pray that you never experience betrayal, but if you have, I pray that you will use it to grow. Do not get revenge. Let them feel or believe that they have won. But know in your heart God had to reveal to you the person you call friend. I thank God for mine because they helped to push me to my next level.

Holding onto that hurt will block your blessings. Love them regardless of how they did you and watch how you will still get blessed.

3.6: The Hole

I had just graduated massage therapy school and was in the field for only a few months before I decided to be an assistant for a hairstylist. At the time, I was really struggling, and I needed some money. The things she needed done, I could do. I was already a licensed master haircare specialist, so I was qualified to help her.

Throughout my time there, all I had was a corner and a chair right beside the dryer and trash can. The chair I used for the clients to sit in was eventually upgraded to a salon chair once the owner decided to make some renovations. Yes, I was the assistant, but I was also the "do girl". I would help everyone in the salon if I could. I would pick up lunch, run their errands, drop their laundry, and even help the other stylists with their clients.

It eventually became the norm and everyone including myself, would expect it. I honestly didn't have problem a with helping it was just a lot sometimes. I wanted that extra money. I was slowly starting to get aggravated because I didn't see myself as an assistant. I am a leader! I was born a leader. Yet becoming an assistant humbled me in many ways. I had learned how to operate and maneuver through what I had. If it wasn't there at the time "oh well" is what I used to get. I was left to figure it out. Left to shut my mouth, humble myself, and get it done. It was moments that it didn't feel good, but it taught me self-control. It taught me how to control my mouth and my reactions. I was never afraid to speak up, but people are always watching, and there were certain impressions of myself that I didn't want to carry with me throughout my life.

About a year had passed when I had reached my breaking point. I was done being an assistant. I was ready to dive into the massage world and learn myself as a massage therapist. I wanted and needed to be free. But something was holding me back. Fear. The unknown. I had got comfortable with the money. I wasn't sure how being a massage therapist was going to turn out. I desired it, but I was scare to dive in. That unknown place had me scared. I was uncomfortable, not happy, and felt unappreciated but, the money was good.

I had started working less days at the salon. One morning, I received a text asking to please come to work and breakfast would be on her. I agreed because I needed the money. I got up, got ready, and met her at the salon. We rode to Chic-fil-A and got breakfast as we talked about something that was currently going on. We talked until her client got there.

We worked a normal busy day. Around noon, I was hungry like always, but I needed to make a run to Walmart. Before I left, we agreed on ordering food from Applebee's. All I wanted was a side salad with a piece of grilled chicken with Ranch and Italian dressing. Usually, I would go pick up the food, but this day one of her friends agreed to pick it up. I was gone 45 minutes because I had seemed my sister's daddy and stopped to talk to him. When I got back, the food wasn't there. I asked her about the food and what happened. She told me her husband went and got her something to eat from Oliver Garden instead. I never got a phone call about the change of plans and I didn't get anything to eat either.

As I was asking her questions, she immediately told me I could have her salad. He then arrives with the food and she proceeds to go outside to eat. Keep in mind, the person currently sitting in her chair asked for some of her food and she agreed to give her some.

When she came back inside, she handed her client the rest of her food and attempted to hand me some bread. I look at the bread, now mad, because I was confused. *Why is she handing me bread when we agreed on the salad?* Walking toward the back, I tell her to put the bread back there, but asking where the salad was? "Oh! I ate out of it. It was nasty too, but I put it on top of the trash can." She said, "You can get it out the trash!"

Instantly, I knew I was being tested. The old Marti'ka wanted to hit her in her mouth for saying something like that to me. Instead, I asked, "Who do you think I am? Yes, I may be struggling and going through right now but that doesn't mean I have to eat out the trash!" I knew then that whatever fear I had; it was now time to let that fear go. Our friendship, work-ship, her assistant was now gone. I could no longer see myself working for someone that told me to eat out the trash.

I did work with her a few more times after that but everything had changed. I completely let go and started my journey as a massage therapist. Six years later, I am no longer an assistant but now a business owner. September of 2021 will make 3 years for Anointed Massage Studio, offering massages, hair services, plus much more!

If I had to do it over again, I would. I learned a lot during my time with her and I am forever grateful. Maybe if she didn't say what she said, I would have kept wasting time and energy in an environment I no longer wanted to be a part of. I was helping to grow someone else business while neglecting the dream God gave me to become a business owner.

God will allow you to go through things to humble you sometimes. I was a person that was always ready. Down for whatever when it came to fighting but not this time. I was forced to think about myself, the environment, and the other people at that moment. So even in my low moment, I discovered that's when God is up to something. He was testing me yet equipping me to be able to withstand and stand even when I may feel like fighting. You must learn how to let God fight your battles for you.

3.7: 6 Plus "One"

It was Mother's Day and everyone that worked in the shops were mothers. It was a total of seven of us that worked in there. Six out of the seven were booth renters. Even though, I had the education and the license just like everyone else, they were actually stylists. I just didn't have the clientele and I wasn't renting a booth. I was just the assistant for one of the stylists that worked in there.

It was about six o'clock in the evening and everyone was still working. One of the stylists stepped out to go to the store. When she returned, she had balloons and a set of individual flowers to give to everyone that worked in the shop. She proceeds to walk around telling each lady "Happy Mother's Day" while handing them their gift. By the time she got around to me, she didn't have any left. She said to me," I'm so sorry Marti'ka, I forgot about you."

At that very moment I wanted to cry. No balloon. No flower. Only "I'm sorry, I forgot about you." Why was I forgotten about? We had all been working together for a least six months now. I asked myself, *was it because I was the assistant? Was it because I didn't have a station like everyone else? All I had was a chair that sat in the corner beside the head dryer and the trash can."* I was now feeling like I wasn't important and didn't even matter.

Maybe it was because of the way I looked when I went to work. I felt like I was nothing and my appearance reflected that. I didn't care about my appearance. I only cared that I was clean.

During a time in my life, I was already feeling extremely low. I didn't care how I looked. My clothes sometimes wouldn't match, and my hair was screaming "Do Me!" I was struggling in all areas of my life; emotionally, physically, mentally, financially, but most importantly spiritually.

A trigger of being left out and not enough went off in my head and in my heart. A thousand different questions, self-assurance thoughts, forgiveness, rage, and hurt all ran through me at one time. Everything that God had shown me wasn't lining up with what I was going through. I was really facing some extremely low times in my life. When this happened, it took everything in me not to lose it. Not to believe it and most definitely not to accept it. I am somebody and I do matter!

But, let me tell you how God works in mysterious ways. My second child's daddy was helping me watch the boys while I was working due to me working long and crazy hours. It was helping to take the load off my mother because she was also working long and crazy hours. We weren't dating and there was no sexual relationship involved. He would just watch them for me if he could.

About 30 minutes later after she was done handing out everyone else gift, he came to the salon to surprise me with a Mother's Day gift. It was a big balloon and a dozen roses. He wanted to show his appreciation for being a great mother to his son but really to both my boys. He told me that he felt something wasn't right, so he decided to surprise me in front of everyone.

I was still holding in the tears from 30 minutes ago that I wanted to shed. I was feeling so unloved that when he surprised me, those very tears rolled down my face. He didn't know what had just happened. He was clueless but he sensed it. God had given him this feeling, this desire to bless me in front of those that hurt me. At the very moment of feeling unworthy, God sent him to me to show me I am worthy. That God hasn't forgotten about me. She had bought them small balloons and one flower, while he bought me a big balloon and 12 roses.

To say this situation didn't hurt would be a lie, but I learned a valuable lesson from it. God will allow you to be in certain situation and to endure certain pain, but He is a never-failing God. I was looking at what everyone else got and questioning God about it in my mind and heart. I wanted a balloon and a flower just like everyone else. I was wanting someone else gifts. Someone else blessing. I just wanted to feel love. I heard in my spirit *"Cheer up! Here I have your gifts and a blessing right here for you!"*

God blessed me with a bigger balloon and more flowers. In that moment, I felt love and undefeated. God had shown up and let me know that He has me. No matter who may try to hurt me or the situation at hand, I belong to Him. Since I belong to Him, He reminded me that He has me in ALL situations that I shall face.

I want to encourage you to find the good in every hurtful situation. It may not feel good, but it is a lesson that you can learn from it. Every pain has its purpose. Every test has a testimony, and every journey has a story. Take each step by step and leave behind the footprints where they need to be. Never desire what someone else has. God has better for you. Forgive people because sometimes they know not what they do. Most importantly, God will give you the desire of your heart, if it is in His will for your life.

3.8: Knowing When To Let Go

Sometimes loving a person is like drinking poison. Only difference is the poison is an instant kill. Loving someone, especially if it is too long a slow kill. I don't know about you, but one of my biggest issues, is accepting people for who they are. I believe there is good in everyone and everyone is innocent until proven guilty.

The issue at hand is when I try to justify a person action or chose to keep them around after they have offended me or mistreated me. I will constantly give a person chance after chance. But "why?" It's not like I am getting something great out of keeping them around, instead I am getting the short end of the stick.

As I fight with myself, I hear God telling me to let them go. Some people aren't worth holding onto especially when they have shown you how they really feel. A few signs to look at are:

1. How does the person treat you?
2. How does the person make you feel?
3. Are you happy around the person/people?
4. Do you feel like you are truly yourself around them?
5. Do you feel like you are limited around them?
6. How does the person/people talk to you? Around family, friends, or in public?
7. Do you feel the person is secretive?
8. Do you feel that the person is keeping information from you?
9. How is public interaction?

10. Is this person a liar and do they lie a lot?

Are you ignoring the red flags? Most of the time when dealing with someone, there are certain signs that a person shows you that they are not for you. Yet we hold on wishing they will change. But I come to tell you that if you are trading in your happy days for your sad ones, it's time to let it go.

No relationship is really worth your happiness. No matter who the person is. If you must decide who to choose. You better choose you! Especially since that person chooses themselves every time. I'm just really learning to just accept people for who they are. Nothing more and nothing less. If there is no good return from this relationship/friendship, and nothing positive is being produced! What is the point of holding onto it?

Be true to you! Let it go and move on! There is something better on the other side!

3.9: Stop Holding On

"Why you always lying to me? Why can't you just keep it real with me? You will tell me one thing, but your actions show something else." I yell at the top of my lungs. Sitting in the edge of the bed drowning in tears because I am tired of the same games and lies. I am over people lying to me. Especially these men. Why can't they just be honest?

Ring. Ring. Ring. Looking down at my phone he was calling back.

"Yes! What you want?" I answered with an attitude.

"Did you just hang up the phone on me like I wasn't talking to you?" He asks sternly.

"What you want?" I asked.

"Why are you hanging up on me? I told you I was coming and will help you. Stop acting like I won't do nothing for you!" He was saying, trying to explain his self.

"Sir. You told me that yesterday, the day before, and the day before that. So, I am trying to figure out when?" I was ready to hang up the phone again because I didn't like what he was saying. Why did I have to ask for help from someone I am dating a thousand times?

"Marti'ka, listen baby. You know I be busy and have a lot going on, but I promise I will do it tomorrow!" He was saying while trying to smooth talk me. "Ba" was the last thing I heard before I hung up the phone again. He was now sounding like my daddy and the rest of the dudes I know. All men aren't the same, but a lot of them are selfish and liars.

Broken promise after broken promises. When does it ever end? It seen like it is a never-ending cycle when it seen like everyone that I connected too kept broken them. Especially the promises that were made to me. More tears continued to fall as he continued to call my phone. Yelling to the top of my lungs, "It's not fair! I don't deserve this!"

Pause.

Let's stop here for a moment. No one wants to be lied too but it was something that I said during the conversation that made to realize something. "You just like my daddy!" I not the only child that has grew up without a daddy. I was not the first and I won't be the last. I cannot except the guy I am dating to be like my daddy, and I shouldn't either. I shouldn't even compare them two but the first hurt I experienced from a man was my daddy. From my childhood to my adulthood, I have dealt with the broken promises from him repeatedly.

I was putting the guys I were dating into a box. A box that made them just like my daddy if they broke their promises. Making it harder for me to trust them or anything that they said. As soon as I realized a promise was broken, they would feel my pain through my words. It wasn't that I couldn't handle the truth, I couldn't handle the lies. Trigging something in me that makes me want to ask questions and figure out why.

I have always wanted to find the answer but that night I realized that I was still trying to hold on to my daddy. I wanted to be daddy's little girl, but I realized that dream would never be. It was now time to learn how to forgive him. Be accountable in myself for allowing myself to carry the hurt so long. Not saying that my boyfriend lying to me is ok but at the same time, he isn't my daddy. And I shouldn't be blaming him for my daddy's actions.

It was time to step up and completely heal. I would never be able to have a loving relationship if I do not allow myself to heal from the pain of my daddy. No man is him so I cannot blame my hurt on someone else. I encourage you, that if you are holding on to hurt you experienced from a parent. Let it go. It is not easy to do but I promise you that only your life is affected from the hurt. Not theirs but yours.

When the promises of tomorrow start looking closer, there are only two choices available: either (1) you will accept what is ahead without holding on to yesterday, or (2) you will stay stuck in yesterday. Stop holding on to those broken promises. Go chase the promises that are "Yes" and "Amen".

3.10: Healing Is Required

Healing is required in order to be made whole. It's needed in order to truly be happy and at peace. It requires wounds to be touched, wounds to be opened, and the truth to be faced. But how can there be true healing when you have to watch your children face some of the same broken pieces you had to face in life?

"In this season of your life, you will be whole!" were the exact words I heard in my spirit during my time of prayer. Wanting to rebel against the word because I know that true wholeness requires the root of pain to be dealt with.

It requires wounds to be touched. Especially those wounds that were never really discussed. The wounds that you thought you overcame because you gotten older. But the pain cuts so deep that it bought some form of shame. Maybe a feeling of being lost, unloved, or even unworthy. The pain was and is just too much pain to bare.

I never understood how this root cause was going to be fixed. How was this supposed to be handled? I even questioned how could true wholeness be, when I watch my boys fight some of the same battles I had to fight? I knew the root cause of my pain. My root was my father. There was this unconditional love that I had for him. Not to say no one else mattered, but all I wanted to do was make my father proud. I wanted to be daddy's little princess and show him that I could do it. That I could reach my goal and do whatever I desired to do or be.

I wondered if my wholeness would ever be complete until one day, I received a phone call from my daddy. He wanted to talk. An actual conversation with no alcohol involved and nobody else around, just me and him. At first, I honestly didn't care to hear what he had to say. I had just gotten home, and I really wanted the moment to myself. I became quiet and listened. I allowed myself to hear him even through my tears. As I was listening to his story, I had a *"Dang this is crazy"* moment. I could understand some of what he was saying. I could relate. I could relate to his pain and even feel it. In that moment, I found myself silently praying over us. Praying that God would heal both our broken heart.

Did God allow me to go through some of those very things to forgive him? To forgive myself. To forgive God. To hear his story and to hear his pain was like hearing my story and hearing my pain. I question the pain my boys have experienced but how can I teach them if I'm not willing to be taught? How can I teach them to forgive if I cannot forgive? How can there ever be growth if I am not willing?

Along this journey of healing and to complete wholeness, I am learning that sometimes you must be willing to put your feelings to the side and hear the other person out. You will soon discover a key to help you reach your healing. Just like you have a story, they do too.

As a child, you want to know what is going on. You want to know the truth and get mad when someone would lie to you. Do you believe if you are an adult, that kids should not know everything at a young age? Some things are better left unsaid until you are old enough to grasp the concept of what really happened. Even through it all, you must learn how to find the good in the situation. You may never get the answers you need or closure. Maybe the other person just does not know how to face their own demons. Just look at it like this, God protects you from the seen and unseen. Sometimes if you knew the truth about would hurt you more if you knew compared to not knowing at all.

True wholeness requires those wounds to be touched, tortured, and burnt. I encourage you to embrace it, so you don't have to keep looking back, wishing for something better. Not all healing comes from talking it out. Some healing comes only through fasting and praying because our battles are not flesh and blood. The battle is spiritual and on your knees is the only way to defeat it.

Allow yourself to learn how to look at things through spiritual eyes and watch how it will change your perspective on the hurt you have faced.

A man without a vision will perished.

> Proverbs 29:18 (KJV)

3.11: Fading Vision

"Marti'ka, what has gotten into you? The Marti'ka I know is a go-getter. You don't even sound the same. Your voice sound so different?" Ms. Karen asked me.

I was sitting on my couch in tears. We had been on the phone for about 30 minutes now and she was getting on me about not being active in my business. Short of word, all I could say was "Yes ma'am!" Now she was breaking down the hours of the day and the week. She was adding up the hours of the day, subtracting the hours of when to sleep and when to work. "10 hours a week! All you have to do is give your business 10 hours a week. Plug in and see how your business will take off" She said.

The tears that were rolling down my face came from her telling me the truth. I had told her that some days I just look up at the sky and that triggered the whole thing. I was now asking myself, *why was I looking up at the sky?* Sometimes I do look up and say "Thank you Jesus" but sometimes I look up with a blank expression. My mind was completely blank. My mind wasn't allowing me to process my future. I had laid out all my goals and my dream for my life. Yet my life wasn't looking so clear. When COVID-19 hit the world, my mind went on shut down with the rest of the world. Prior to Covid, I'd started a habit of spending money and traveling. I finally had the opportunity to not work while still getting paid.

I didn't have a care in the world. I felt so free. I felt something that I had never felt before. It appears as if I was living in my future. One day I will be able to go as I please, with no worries in the world. Bills paid. Money in my savings. Investing. Kids good. Life is good. I'm gone and away from here, traveling the world with no regrets.

I had a glance of my future, yet I was also being checked. Why have I allowed this time to just relax? I used this time to do absolutely nothing but pay bills and travel. I had allowed my mind to enter a place with nothing, no words, or anyone else actions could phrase me. I was living with no worries. I wasn't concerned about absolutely nothing. I was at peace with myself and my current situation. But this was only temporary because the reality of it all, I still had a lot of work to do.

Where had my vision gone too? How is my mind free yet cloudy at the same time? These were questions that I had asked myself with no answer at all. All I knew was that my vision was fading away and it was now time to tap back into reality. To get back focus on making sure my vision becomes my reality.

Life will have your mind cloudy, but you must learn how to fight through the cloudiness in order to make your vision come to life.

3.12: Me vs. Me

(Scream)

As I look into the mirror, I hear in my head

You ugly

You stupid

No one will ever love you

You will never amount to anything

Constant.

Over and over again

I feel no one loves me

My daddy walked out

My momma was barely there

Family didn't understand me

And my friends….

(Stop, look out into the crowd) (Look back at the mirror)

Well, I don't have no friends

The ones I got close too

Stabbed me in the back

Lied on me or crossed me

I felt alone

I felt no one was there

So, I look in the mirror

Questioning myself,

Asking myself, "Who am I?"

Wondering if my promise will ever become true

I need to fill this void

I need to feel love

So, I settle just to fit in

Settling for less

Just to ease the pain

There was no real love

No real friends

My heart was slowly closing in

How could God bring me into this world

To endure so much pain

How could the ones that's supposed to love me

Hurt me?

I just need help.

I just need to understand.

To say I'm prefect would be a lie

Truth be told

Perfection isn't real

It doesn't exist

It's just a word used for comfort

Comfort to please the flesh

To you it's prefect, if it's right to you

But what is right when we looking through different lenses?

Answer me?

Tell me something?

(Looking crazy) Tell me something now!

(Mirror turns) (Look back with a straight face)

STOP.

STOP.

STOP. Right now!

STOP. This Instant.

See you letting the hurt and words of others

To determine who you are

You better get it together

You a Queen

The daughter of the Most High

Yes life hurts

It will get you down

But you can't let it keep you there

There may never be "I'm sorry" "Please forgive me"

Instead you may get nothing at all

You can't let that hurt consume you

Please forgive. Please let go.

Only you can stop you girl.

Even though life will have you looking at others for help

You need to know to look up instead

It's doesn't matter what those voices say

If it doesn't line up with what God say

"IT DOESN'T MATTER"

Those words can't win

Their actions can't stop you

This is a battle between you and you

Only you can decide

Who are you?

Who do you believe?

I don't know about you but those voices can go head

Everybody isn't meant to stay

Learn. Plant. Grow

Pick your head up

Wear your crown

Loving every inch of you

With pride and dignity

Through the blood, sweat, and tears

Fight.

Smile while fighting to confuse the enemy

Put a praise on it

And go!

It happened.

Forgive. Let go.

It's time to move forward

The love and power you need is in you

Look deep within and find yourself.

Without looking for the answers from others

Look up and within

Yes, it happened but what's next?

If you don't mind me asking?

I must walk, hike, climb, and conqueror each mountain to truly enjoy the view up top.

----Marti'ka Strong

Section Four:

I Must Fight!

My Dream Is On the Line

If life is the reason, you haven't move yet, then you don't understand the definition of life.

(Essay written for a scholarship in 2015)

Explosive Desire

Growing up, my three bedrooms house in Rock Hill, South Carolina, was home to everyone. I not only grew up in one of the roughest neighborhoods in the city, but also lived in a house full of people. Even those that weren't family lived in the same house from time to time. Waking up every day with a house full of people was like opening a can of sardines.

There was never any room in the house for all those people, but no one ever wanted to go home because my house was like home to them. I was constantly surrounded by people, yet I still felt like an outsider. I lived in a fantasy world majority of my childhood. I constantly was looking towards the stars, reading, and finding different ways to become smarter. I wanted to better myself and to find ways to get out of the hood. I never dreamed of living in the hood my entire life, only doing my childhood years where I could not make a decision on my own.

I am the middle child of my mother's three children, and I am like oil and water with the other two. To me, I was a leader and was never afraid to go after what I genuinely wanted. While my sister may be entertaining my friends, cousins, or brother, I was sitting in my own world dreaming about my future. I knew in my heart that one day I would be someone great. I would be someone so great that I would leave behind a legacy that would impact generation after generation. I remember as a little girl when I would come home from school, I would play teacher all by myself. I would teach the air because I did not have anyone to attend, not even my baby dolls and stuff animals. It was just me, my teaching assignment, and my easel board. Looking back over that period in my life, I see that I was determined to succeed. I was determined to be successful. I was determined to keep going regardless of who was listening or paying attention. I believe in me even when no one else understood me.

Waking up every morning is surely a blessing and I thank God for the chance to wake up to impact the next person I may see. God is the reason that I have overcame so many obstacles in my life that has tried to kill me, break me, and make me give up. When I am weak, He is strong, so I know He is the reason I can still go on. Out of the 25 years of my life, as a single mother with two young boys, my dreams never stopped. It seems as if the more hurt, pain, confusion, lies, and people turned against me, I was motivated to prove everyone wrong. It gave me a drive that only pushed me and not stop me.

I have always had the gift of doing hair but so for long I ran from it because I could not see myself being a hairstylist for my career. I wanted to be different. I wanted to think outside of the box and choose a career that a lot of people in my ethic group did not have a desire to do. Finally, after running from my gift for so long, I decided to go to school, complete the program, and I graduated in January 2015. It took me almost nine years to complete the program because I could not see myself in the field. In between my breaks from that program, I attended different schools searching for pieces that were not a clear picture in my life. After I graduated from high school, I attended York Technical College, worked two-part times jobs, and raised my oldest son. I completed that program in May of 2011. I also obtain my health and life insurance license in which I worked in the health field for three years. In the mist of trying to find the correct direction, I found out I was pregnant with my second child. I still felt like something was missing, so I attempted two other colleges trying to receive my bachelor's degree, in which I still do not have. It was me running from my future, from God's will, His purpose for my life that I felt like I was missing pieces in my life. I felt that my career was not going the way I wanted it to go. Once I decided to stop running and walk into destiny, doors started opening. My life changed.

I attended Southeastern Institute to study Professional Clinical Massage Therapy because I believe in hands that can still heal. I believe that I can make a difference or help someone that is in pain to feel better. Knowing that I would be making a difference in someone else life would bring joy to my heart. After I complete this program, it will allow me the opportunity to build my empire. My dream is to one day become a billionaire, owning a lot of different business, and impacting the world in different ways. Completing and receiving license or degrees in the other fields will allow me the opportunity to start a business where it would be considered a one stop shop. You will be able to get your hair done or cut, purchase insurance, and massages for enjoyment or medicate purposes just to name a few.

I believe in my heart that education should not have an age limit on it. The age you learn to start reading or learning should never be a question, but are you willing and ready to continue learning despite your age? I believe in my heart that knowledge is power. My dreams, visions, and goals are so huge; I must always educate myself.

Benjamin Franklin, one of our country's founders, was a dreamer who left behind a life changing legacy. He not only was a leader, inventor, writer but he was a visionary. He dreamed and because he dreamed, he impacted the world from generation to generation.

Benjamin Franklin quoted many aphorisms which was short and straight to the point statements. He once said if a man empties his purse into his head, no man can take it away from him. An investment in knowledge always pays the best interest.

Even when people were laughing at me about receiving my education and attending school, I kept pushing. I knew that what I envisioned to do in life would require all the education I could get. Investing into my brain, expanding my mind and knowledge has been one of the best choices I have ever made in my life. I know that one day it will all pay off and I shall leave behind a legacy that will change the world forever.

4.1: The Skies Has No Limit

It was a beautiful sunny day and my grandfather and I, were sitting outside on the porch. Enjoying the breeze while listening to the bird's chirp. Looking up at the sky, daydreaming about my future. Thinking of different ways, I was going to impact the world.

"Marti'ka!" my grandfather called my name.

"Yes sir?" I answered with excited in my voice. I loved my grandfather. He was the father that I never had. He loved on me and gave me a lot of knowledge at such a young age.

He slowly turned towards me "Marti'ka, you can be whatever you want to be." He said to me.

"I know I can papa! I want to be a teacher one day. I want to be someone that will make a difference in the world." I told my grandfather as I started to stare at the sky.

"Well guess what baby, you already are making difference in this world. It bought so must joy to my heart when I saw you teaching in your room the other day. To see you at such a young age, you are most definitely a young lady with a great mind. Remember Marti'ka the skies have no limits when God is involved. Trust that He will carry you through every obstacle that you may face in life. Never forget that."

My grandfather was now looking into my eyes as he talked to me. He wanted to make sure that I truly understood what he was telling me. Even though I was only about five years old, my grandfather seems that my future was bright.

"Never let anyone tell you that you can't because you can!" He said with a slight laugh but with a serious tone. "Yes, papa! I hear you but why you are laughing?" I asked.

"Baby girl I heard that word "can't" so many times growing up so I'm sitting here with you today to tell you that you can. Grabbing my hand, he smiled as we enjoyed the beautiful moment on the porch. I didn't realize at the time that my grandfather was giving me some very important advice for life.

It took a while before I truly understood what my grandfather was telling me but now, I know to trust and believe my dream. To trust the process. "Can't" isn't a word that should be in your vocabulary. Instead, "I can!" should be the correct words to use.

Trust in the dream of your heart and trust that you can do it with Christ Jesus!

4.2: My Dreams Shall Come True

You may not be like Daniel in the bible (Daniel 1:17) "having understanding in all visions and dreams" but if you are dreaming; a lot can be revealed to you through your dreams. So, what exactly are dreams? Well dreams are:

- a series of thoughts, visions, or feelings that happen during sleep.
- an idea or vision that is created in your imagination and is not real.
- something that you have wanted very much to do, be, or have for a long time.

I believe dreaming of things you want to accomplish in life can help both while you are asleep and while you are awake. Either way, dreaming can truly be effective if you allow yourself to listen and take actions if needs be.

When dreaming while asleep, there can be lots of things revealed to you - your past, present, and even your future." Peoples' intentions can also be revealed in dreams as well. Writing your dreams down could be helpful where you may need to reflect on it later in life.

Now if you are daydreaming, Habakkuk 2:2 states "Write the vision; make it plain." So, I encourage you to write it down, believe in your dream and run for it. A few things I do while chasing my dreams are:

- I pray and talk to God

- I read and educate myself on the subject

- I stay positive

- I speak with confidence
- I encourage myself to stay strong
- I accept the good and the bad
- I am always aware of my attitude
- I am always open to learn

These are only a few things that I did that has helped me to push through. Most importantly, talk to God about your dreams whether it occurred while you were sleep or if you were daydreaming about something so you can get the correct answer in return.

4.3: I Dream Like Him

Martin Luther King Jr once said, "And so even though we face the difficulties of today and tomorrow, I still have a dream." I have always admired how he walked in life.

After learning about him, I realized that I was a little girl that had a dream just like him. I didn't understand life and what was going to come but I knew something was. Everything wasn't always going to be gravy. Troubles was going to come but I was determined no matter what to reach my goal ahead. His story taught me that it doesn't matter what storm you are facing in life, you never stop dreaming. In fact, you dream harder and fight like never before.

I have always daydreamed about being someone great that would help change the world. Just like Martin Luther King Jr. I even gave myself a nickname, Martin Luther King Jr Jr Jr Jr, but the female version. Leaving behind a legacy that's going to change the world forever. Helping to save the upcoming generations to come.

While his dream was to bring unity in America, I dream of saving souls and talking about Jesus. Helping people to become free from their past to truly live. To encourage people to chase their dreams regardless of what they see and to live life with complete fullness.

Life doesn't stop when things get hard. Instead, life keeps running its course rather you are here or not. Never allow yourself to stop dreaming because life seems hard. Never allow fear to turn you away or stop you. Fear is not of God, but freedom and courage are.

Fight for your dreams no matter how unrealistic it seems to you. What seems unrealistic to you is for sure realistic to God if it's in His will.

It takes more energy to give up and be unhappy, then it does to fight and be happy.

4.4: My Dream Show Me Things

Have you ever had a dream while sleeping that it seems as if you were there? You remember where you were at and even the colors that you had on. Your dream was so detailed that you could tell someone else while painting a clear picture.

Well, I can relate to you if you have. I know what it's like to dream something as if I was there. Yet, I'm sound asleep while my conscience is dreaming of whatever.

In my early teens, I met a girl through a guy I was dating at the time. We were around her daily and we became close with each other. Due to where we stayed, we attended different schools and started making new friends.

Years passed and we reconnected again. We started hanging out, cooking at her house, and playing cards to catch up on all the lost times. I felt that I had my friend back until one day she told me her and my baby daddy had been talking for about a month.

I was lost for words and hurt. We weren't together anymore, and she wasn't my best-friend, but I still considered her a friend and he is my child father. Why would they do this though? I felt like I was being stabbed in my back because I knew they knew about me. She told me she was going to keep talking to him because we weren't that close anymore. We had just cooked fish and shrimp at her house a week prior.

They eventually started dating and moved in together. That family that we had no longer existed because he was now starting a new family with now an old friend. I couldn't even be happy because I desired my family that he never wanted from the beginning.

A few months in after they started dating, she became pregnant. I was crushed even more. I didn't understand how he could pay bills somewhere else and help her with her kids and not help with his own son. Then to make another one and he wasn't taking care of his son.

I had a lot of sleepless nights because of the situation. I still desired my family, and I felt so betrayed. I had to pray constantly for God to give me strength and to heal my heart. Give me strength to forgive both and move on with my life.

One night I had a dream where the girl was going to apologize to me for hurting me. Trying to make things right so she could move forward with her life. God let me know not to worry and gave me the comfort I needed.

About six months or a year later, she apologized to me because she lost the baby and needed the closure to move on. I needed the same closure as well. I let her know I was sorry for her lost and I accepted her apologize. I needed and wanted to move on with my life, I couldn't hold on any longer.

God let me know in my dream that I was going to receive the closure I was looking for. I just didn't understand the situation and why it had to happen to me. But one thing I have learned is you have to be careful of the choices you make because karma has no target. Except for those that doesn't release it.

I said all that to say this, dreams can come in different ways to show you different things. Never question your dreams, instead tap into them.

4.5: The Courage To Stand

Courage isn't something that occurs overnight. It takes time to build courage to tackle each level that you are trying to achieve. So, what exactly is the definition of courage:

-the ability to do something that frightens one.
-strength in the face of pain or grief.

Do you have the courage and the strength you need to succeed while chasing your career? Achieving success won't be easy but you must have the courage to sustain. Having courage is sometimes harder than it sounds, but the first step is to try to accomplish something that you think about.

If you never try, then you will never know how much courage you have or even if you have a breaking point. Regardless, if you like your mountain or not, each mountain will require you to achieve another level of courage. So, what choice do you make? Do you stand and fly like the eagle? Or do you cluck and walk like the chickens? Deuteronomy 31:6 states "Be strong and of a good courage, fear not, nor be afraid of them: for the Lord thy God, he it is that doth go with thee; he will not fail thee, nor forsake thee."

I say to you regardless of what you face, you need courage to stand.

4.6: I Need Courage Spiritually Too

Have you ever experienced rejection from others? Family, friends, or even church members? There were times when you reached out to people for help, and they weren't there for you? Whether it is to help solve a problem or watch your kids, just so you can form a better life. Better yet, have you ever been rejected for just being yourself.

The feeling of been rejected isn't easy but you must continue to chase your dreams, even when everyone around you has rejected you.

I once experienced a hurt from my church. I was at a point in life where I felt like my pastor didn't care about me. He didn't really care about what I was going through. He didn't care about what I could bring to the church to help. I felt that I was been overlooked. I felt like the church that I had dedicated two years of my life too didn't appreciate me.

One Sunday, the pastor said that people would start having dreams that would concern the church and the people in the church. That same night, I had a weird dream that involved the pastor, his mother – the copastor, the church, and myself. I first spoke with his mother about it, and she said talk to him because she wasn't sure.

I then tried to reach him three times in person, through text, and messenger and still no response. I wondered why he didn't want to hear my dream if he just stated that people would start having them about the church. I had one so why ignore me?

I prayed about it repeatedly trying to find the answer. God let me know He was allowing it to happen to build me up for my ministry. To help me with the next level He was taking me. Even tough God gave me the answer to my question, I was still trying to find closure in the entire situation, but I couldn't.

I allowed myself to get mad at the church and even at God. I felt like the people that was supposed to be there to support, encourage, and push me to the next level spiritually didn't even truly care about me. I left church and I left God too.

See, I didn't have enough courage to still stand even after God told me what the deal was with entire situation. I still allowed my feelings to have control instead of God having control of the situation. So, I ran from what God was telling me because I didn't want to accept His answer.

I allowed an answer that I didn't want to stop my walk with God. When in fact, I should have been thankful that God was allowing me to see, know, and understand the entire situation. I blamed God and the pastor for my rejection when it was only God protecting me.

To stand when you have experienced hurt from others is one thing, but to experience it from your church is different. I didn't know how to stand. There was no courage in me to continue to go to church, pray, fast, and talk to God because I felted rejected. I ran away instead of having courage to stand.

I know the feeling of rejection while trying to figure out the next steps in life. I know the feeling of hurt and the pain that cuts deep. I really gave up in some situations allowing the distractions to steal a portion of my courage that I have.

Through it all I had to forgive everyone in the situation including God. For me to move forward to the next journey. I honestly do not regret it because I learned that if I allowed a person to interfere with my relationship with God to stop me then what kind of relationship do I truly have with Him?

4.7: I Had To Graduate

My story of hair is long and aggravating. I started doing hair when I was in the 2nd grade, but it was something about hair that I couldn't accept it all the way. When I started braiding, I was one of the few braiders around my age that did hair. I made some money doing it throughout my years, but I could never love it. I never had that drive to commit to it and never dreamed of it as my career. As I got older more people around me started to do hair and fell in love with it, but I never could.

I have tried a million times to walk away from it, but it always seemed to come back around to me. I started taking Cosmetology classes at ATC in 2006, my 11th grade year of high school. I got pregnant into second semester, so I wasn't able to attend my senior year and finish the course. I tried to enroll at Empire Beauty School in 2011 but something with my financial aid delayed me a month. I withdrew and signed up for my bachelor's degree instead.

That didn't work, so in 2012, I enrolled into barber/hair school. I'm not sure how long I was there before I withdrew and went to another barber/hair school. Once I started the new school, I only went for about 6 weeks before I withdrew to go to work full time. The full-time job was only temporary, so I was right back in school in March 2014.

By this time, I was behind a lot of hours and the two people I started with were no longer in my class. When I tell you March 2014-January 2015 were some very trying and testing months for me. I had to deal with a lot of attitudes, nick picking, and learning nothing at all.

There were times I would get laughed at because I was curious about Jesus. I would rather do my biblical studies instead of sitting around talking. Bored in class one day, I wrote Ms. Millionaire Strong on all my books and it seem like everyone had something to say because I dreamed beyond a barber shop.

One day, we were given a project to complete a layout for our business. I completely designed my business laying it out from the square footages to the colors. Which the business consists of barber, hair, massages, my book, a classroom, and a store.

I was teased and questioned because they wanted to know how I was going to do it. I was never at school, so to them, my completion was impossible. Honestly to me, my completion was impossible as well. Yet I never told them I wasn't going to finish. My argument was always, "It doesn't matter what you say, I'm going to graduate."

As January approached, the month of graduation, I was extremely nervous because I didn't know if I was going to graduate. I was down about 500 hours, and I needed those hours to finish. Luckily, at the previous barber/hair school, I had collected enough hours so my hours could transfer. The entire month of January I was on pins and needles, but I never let them know. To them, I was graduating even when I was ready to quit a few weeks before graduation.

I received my hours just in time for me to walk the stage. Even though I fought with them and my mind about graduation, I still fought through to prove I could. I had to prove to them, and God had to prove to me He could.

I knew it was only God that pushed me through because if it were up to me, I would have given up. I learned to fight for something that could help me and hurt me even when I didn't want too.

My journey of trying to become a licensed stylist was challenging because I fought against it for so long. I realized I had to push through because I made it too far to walk away. Stopping was no longer an option. I had to finish for me, for my kids, and for the people God may place along the way.

When I finally completed everything, it gave me a joy no man could give and faith no man could shake. God really showed me Himself during the process and I thank Him for it. He taught me how to finish the race even when I wanted to give up.

So that dream or goal you trying to accomplish, ask yourself, are you going to accomplish it or are you going to give up?

4.8: Dedication Is Important

I believe everyone in life go through a phrase where people are telling them they must dedicate themselves to something. You need to dedicate to this and that only to find yourself unsure of what to dedicate your life too. Dedication is:

-the quality of being dedicated or committed to a task or purpose.

-the action of dedicating a church or other building.

I learned from experience to never allow any man to have control over your dedication in your life. I will instruct thee and teach thee in the way which thou shalt go: I will guide thee with mine eye (Psalm 32:8) (KJV).

Dedication requires you to keep fighting and going even when you want to give up. Even when it does not work right or make you take an extra turn. You must keep going!

It took me a while before I was truly able to grasp the true definition of dedication but once I did, I realized it only made me stronger. True dedication made me appreciate the storm so much more.

4.9: I Made It Baby

It was March 2015, and I was starting massage therapy classes at Southeastern Institute. Only a month in between graduating hair school to massage school, I was determined to get this under my belt. I had fell in love with the muscles of the body and how the body operates.

I did not have any Pell grant money left for school and my loan amount was adding up. I needed $15,000 for school and all I had to offer was $492, the rest of my Pell money. I wasn't really working so I couldn't afford to pay the school either. I won a $2,000 scholarship to help knock the balance down, but it still was not enough. Yet, I came to school every day determined to complete these courses and with honors.

Everyone in the house was in school so not only did I have to manage the house, my schoolwork but help my boys with their schoolwork as well. I had a full load on my hands.

I was going into my 4th month finishing up the first 3 months with A's when one early morning I got a life changing phone call. My oldest son's father had been shot 3 times in the throat. Not knowing how this entire situation was about to play out, my first thought was to drop out of school. I felt like I was not going to be able to handle this pressure and successfully pass my classes. My mind was now extra cloudy.

Regardless of what me and him had gone through, he could trust that he will always have a friend. This was a moment that I felt he needed me. I had been there through a lot of other things and him fighting for his life, was no different.

I remember arriving at the hospital to see him wrapped up and a hole in his throat. As bad as I wanted to know what happen, I knew he couldn't talk. I did find out he was shot twice not three times though. Still thinking how I am going to explain this to my baby, but I was thankful that he was still here. I had just lost a best friend exactly 11 months from the date he was shot. To lose him would have been too much to bear.

I prayed over him and trusted that God had him because He allowed him to still be here. I was there as much as I could because I know he needed me. Not as the mother of his child, not as a girlfriend but as a friend. As a friend that had been riding this wave with him since we met in 2005.

I had made the decision to withdraw from class and come back next month until I realized that I wouldn't be graduating in October. Instead, I would be graduating in November, but it would be after my birthday. My birthday gift to myself was to graduate, pass my MBLEX, and become a license massage therapist.

As much as I loved him and wanted to be there every day, I couldn't. I had to complete my classes and graduate on time. During that month and the next month after, I got B's in my classes, but I did finish my last 2 classes with A's.

Those first three months seemed to go by smoothly but as I approached the finish line, I was distracted to throw me off course. Even though I didn't take that break, I was very close to it. I was so close that I was about to allow the enemy to win. I was about to allow him to try and take away something I finally loved to do and that was becoming a massage therapist.

I had to come back to the reality of life. Life will happen, but you cannot allow it to consume you. You cannot stop or give up just because it's not working the way you want it too. You will never allow yourself to make it. You must push past that mountain to reach the top.

I didn't graduate with the Highest Honors, but I did graduate with Honors finishing massage therapy school with 6 A's and 2 B's. I was still determined because I had found my passion in the love of massaging muscles.

Determination will take you farther then dreaming it will. You can dream it all day, but you must be determined in order to accomplish it. I encourage you to dream with determination to finish the race.

4.10: My Dedication Is Not In Vain

Stated previously in the other chapters, I talked about my adventure with all my degrees and certification. I really went on a career roller coaster trying to find happiness in my career. I already knew that I wasn't going to be going to work every day without having the chance to say I found my career-a career that I loved.

I was determined to find the career I love, which took a lot of dedication to keep pushing forward even when I wanted to give up. Over the years of hopping from career to career, I didn't have a steady job by choice, I wasn't able to live the life I wanted, and my kids missed out because I couldn't afford it.

My last go round of school, I found my passion. I found a career that I felt was promising to me which made it promising for my kids. They didn't have to hear mommy mouth everyday about a job I couldn't stand or things I could not afford at that moment.

I refused to settle when it came to my career. I stayed dedicated, even as I soared through each storm. I didn't allow my storms to stop me. They may have hindered me but never stop me because storms are a part of life.

Now, I know some may say I am selfish to my kids in which to a certain extent I may have been. Yet, when you see a bigger picture ahead that is truly clear, you start planning. I needed to show my boys, it's ok to chase your dreams. I must be their first explain, not anyone else. I needed for them to see if my mother can do it at a young age and alone, I can do it too. Regardless, of any situation.

Understand that you can't reach your tomorrow without been prepped from your yesterday. Every day has a story, it's just up to you and how you play or replay it.

4.11: Success Isn't Overnight

If you're trying to become successful overnight, let me help you real quick: stop thinking that it will be a quick process because it won't. True success takes time, sweat, failure and tears. A lot of people say that they want to be successful in life, but don't quite understand everything that comes with success. The definition of success is:

-the accomplishment of an aim or purpose.

-the attainment of popularity or profit.

-a person or thing that achieves desired aims or attains prosperity.

Everyone has different things they want to accomplish in life. Looking at what you are trying to accomplish, do you consider yourself successful at what you do? Or are you on the path to become successful in your career or your life, period?

Understand that success is not easy, but it must be done. Being unhappy and unwilling to accept your past choices makes it harder to move forward to truly attained your success. Remember the good chapters of your life to help with your future decisions while erasing the negative ones. Do not worry, for worrying cannot change anything. And never stop striving for your success.

4.12: I See My Success

I have told you about certain things I had to face in my life, but I never allowed it to determine if I would be successful or not. For example, I was labeled as a statistic when I got pregnant with my oldest son. I was told that I would not be able to complete certain things because I was a teenage mother. When I got pregnant with my second son, my oldest son's daddy once mentioned signing over my rights because he felt I could not raise two kids at 22 years old. Even watching all my friends drop out of school or given up on their dreams, I kept pushing.

I have put my hands in a few different fields because I told myself I would not limit my chance of learning and having different things under my belt (I will always have something to fall back on if one thing doesn't work).

I went from a mother my senior year to graduating first semester in 2007. I started York Technical College in the fall of 2008 in criminal justice, later changing it to Business Administration specializing in Paralegal. Soon graduating in May 2011 with my associate degree. In between 2011 to 2013, I tried to get my bachelor's degree, but it fell through every time. I found myself enrolled in barber school in 2013, dropping out for 6 months only to find myself right back to complete what I started. I graduated from there January 2015, only to find myself in massage therapy school from March 2015 to October 2015. Oh, and along the journey of all these degrees, I got my life and health license as well.

I know you probably thinking *why she got all these degrees and certification*, but I was determined to find the career that I would love. My success along the way didn't come from having all these different degrees and certification but from my failures, my pain, long nights, and the rain. I found my love for massage therapy, my very last choice.

I was thought of as someone that couldn't. As someone that would never amount to anything or just doing too much. Failure wasn't an option for me and since I seem my mother slave for someone else company, I was determined to make a change.

I was a young mother lost in life. Learning to raise my boys, love me, and deal with this world was truly a lot for me. Being a mother is a job all alone but with two hyper yet very smart and handsome men. I promise you I have messed up so many times. "For a just man falleth seven times, and riseth up again" (Proverbs 24:16)(KJV). But every time, I fell I promised myself that I wouldn't stay down there.

I don't care what your current situation looks like, you must keep pushing. If you determined your success off what others call successful, then you will never value your success. I encourage you to never allow your yesterday to determine your tomorrow. Reach constantly until you reach your promise of your tomorrow!

4:13: Success Comes By Hearing

As the leader of the Israelites, Joshua was successful at knocking down the walls of Jericho because he listened and followed God's commands.

I believe that everyone has a desire to be successful in life, but life sometimes gets the best of us. Success doesn't come quickly, and there will be many nights of lost sleep as we work and burn the midnight oil. Regardless of what Joshua had to endure, he was determined to hear and listen to God to be successful.

I started writing this book in 2009 because I used to send out inspirational text messages every day. I had someone to encourage me to turn it into a book. It's 2021 and the book is just being release. I have written this book over and repeatedly.

It started off inspirational, to using acronyms, to using those words talking about others life, ending talking completely about me. Plenty of nights, months, years, that I walked away from my book, only to return to it. It was a struggle to write this book, but throughout it all my life was transiting so it couldn't have been completed. There were still things that needed to be said.

It took 11 plus years to complete this book, but I never gave up on my dream of becoming an author one day. No, I may not be a well-known author yet but there was a form of success completed. I finally completed my book with the help of others. From the things said and done toward me, I was able to turn my pain into a story. Most importantly, allowing my ears to be open when God said *work on your book*.

Success requires a lot of listening, learning, and trying. Despite any fears, worries, or uncertainties, you must be determined to reach that end goal. Are you willing to listen and hear from God to be successful in your career or life overall?

Growth occurs when you realize that your tomorrow is determined by your yesterday.

-Marti'ka Strong

Section Five:

Spiritual Growth:

My Flesh Can't Win Forever

Your flesh can't always be first, instead you should let your spirit lead.

5.1: Prayer Changes Things

Constantly, I hear people say I need prayer or please pray for me because I am going through. Trying to find peace in their situation they reach out for someone else to stand in agreement with them about their current situation.

Do you believe prayer still can work and change any situation? Prayer provides a way to set yourself free from all worries. The definition of prayer is:

-a solemn request for help or expression of thanks addressed to God.
-a religious service, especially a regular one, at which people gather to pray together.
-an earnest hope or wish.

According to 1 Kings 9:3 "And the Lord said unto him, I have heard thy prayer and thy supplication, that thou hast made before me: I have hallowed this house, which thou hast built, to put my name there forever; and mine eyes and mine heart shall be there perpetually." When we take the time to pray to God, He hears our requests.

Prayer should not be because you need God during your time of troubles instead it should be a daily, constant time with God. Prayer can sometimes just consist of thanking God for who He is or His grace and mercy.

Yet, God is a loving Father that we can pray about whatever and whoever. He wants us to pray about everything and be anxious about nothing (Philippians 4:6-7). Never run from prayer or feel that it does not work. That one special prayer can change your life for a lifetime.

5.2: Prayer Has Changed Me

There are a lot of people who do not believe in the power of prayer. Because of this, they see no point in praying. But I can tell you from experience that prayer can change things in your life.

Growing up, I have always had a heart of gold but a mean streak and disrespectful mouth that attacked anyone I felt was rude towards me. I was a very outspoken person and did not care how my words may have affected others. When I was angry, my feelings were the only thing that mattered. But having that mindset only caused hurt, regret, and sorrow, and soon my own rash words were used against me.

As I got older and started to mature, I recognized that my tongue needed to be tamed. I began to pray for God to humble me and control my tongue. Your tongue can be the nastiest thing on your body if you do not learn how to control it. And while the process of taming your words is not always easy, I can promise you the result is worth it. While there are still some days when I must stop myself from talking, I thank God that my mouth is not the same. I am more aware of the things I say. Sometimes it really Is best to just smile and say nothing if you have nothing nice to say.

Prayer can also help us break away from addictions, such as an addiction to fornication. But understand that I am still in the process of putting this bad habit behind me. Even though our prayers are always answered, your desire is rarely granted overnight, either because the time is not right or because of our own failings. And that is why I am speaking from a position of transition.

I started having sex at the age of 13. Even at such a young age, I believed it was something that I must have. I hardly went a day without having sex. The only time I did not have sex was during my menstruation, but that depended on the day as well. It was like a drug to me, and before long I was addicted. My sex addiction led me to choose to open doors that God did not plan for my life.

By the time I reached my mid-twenties, I was tired of the hurt, pain, and disappointment from having sex with men who were just my boyfriends or just someone I was having sex with. I was done with settling for less than what God had for me. I started praying against the spirit of fornication and asked God to deliver me from it. As the days passed and I continued to pray, I slowly started losing the desire for sex and I did not crave it as often. Having it every day soon became every other day, leading to only once a week, followed by once a month, and then even less than that. After 3 free months I fell, but I had accomplished something that I thought was near impossible.

I need you to understand that God delivered me from fornication, but I opened that door back up. Yet I can honestly say that those were the 3 peaceful months of my life that I could remember. Why? There was no sexual attachment to anyone. It did not bother me if John did not call because I wasn't giving him my body. I was not giving up my soul only to get nothing in return aside from a passing minute of pleasure.

I encourage everyone to take your situation and troubles to the throne of God and leave them there. We have souls, so we fight against spirits, not flesh. And when we fight, Christ Jesus can deliver and heal us from anything through prayer.

Prayer does make a difference. If you believe that Jesus can do it, then it shall be done. Pray mindfully and from the heart, seeking to do the will of God, and He will give you what your heart desires.

5.3: Prayer Healed Me Last Night

There are different levels of faith in God. I have always believed in God. Yet, while I trusted Him to have a path planned for my life, I didn't trust that prayer could really heal someone else, better yet myself. But I learned in September of 2010 that God still hears our prayers, and He still heals.

It was a Friday in September of 2010 and I was sick. I was working at the local Wal-Mart Supercenter in the photo lab. I was supposed to be going out to party with one of my co-workers in the electronics department for his birthday. While I wasn't sure if I could make it, I still told my friend that I would try to go out with him since I had promised him.

After my shift ended, I went home and took my temperature; the thermometer read 100 degrees. Shocked by the number, I immediately took some medicine and went to bed. When I woke up 3 hours later, I felt a little better, so I got ready and headed out. However, by the time I drove to his house, I was tired and sluggish again, hardly able to move. I called it quits and turned around, driving straight back down the highway, heading straight for home and bed.

When I woke up the next morning, I was running a temperature of 102. My body had an ache that dug down to my bones. And while I managed to drive to work, I slept once I got there, leaning up against the counter. I didn't even have enough energy to stand up straight. Three hours into my shift, I called it a day and left.

When I finally got back home, I took my temperature again; it was 101 degrees. I fell into bed and slept and slept, only waking up to take pills and check my temperature. It was constantly changing and not for the better.

About ten o'clock that night, my boyfriend at the time was alarmed by my condition and tried to rouse me, "Marti'ka, get up. Move, please. Baby, what's wrong? Talk to me, please!" However, I couldn't move or speak. The pain was so severe; it was hard for me to open my eyes. When I managed to take my temperature, it read 103.

The medicine wasn't working, so I prayed that night for God to remove whatever my body was fighting inside of me. I told Him I was putting it all in His hands. I wasn't completely confident He would heal me, but I knew He was in control.

When I woke up the next morning, I had no pain, and my temperature was back to normal. God was still in the healing business. Thanks to Him, my body was free from the temperature and pain, and my mind was renewed. I sang all day long, full of joy that did not cease.

God opened my eyes and showed me that He could heal anything if I trusted and believed in Him. Now I know that I am not alone. I didn't need to see a doctor to cure my pain; God cured it for me.

5.4: Jesus Wasn't An Option

"Get up, Marti'ka. It's time to get ready for church!" My grandma yelled into my room because this was probably her third time telling me to get up. "Yes ma'am." I said with a low and raspy voice. I was sleeping good and didn't want to move but my grandma always made sure we were at church every Sunday morning. Taking a glance at the white and pink dress hanging up in my closet, I still could not decide which dress I wanted to wear.

I walked to the bathroom only to smell the aroma of bacon, grits, and eggs that had already been cooked. "Hurry up so you can eat and get ready. I called your name three times this morning young lady." My grandma said as she looked at me like *you playing around on this Sunday morning*. I hurried into the bathroom to use it, wash my face, and brush my teeth. I only had about 15 minutes before the van arrived for me to eat and get dress. I rushed out the bathroom to the table to eat.

"Slow down now Marti'ka before you choke on your food." My grandma said as she walked into the kitchen. "I'm trying to hurry up, so I can be ready when the van arrives granny." Answering with a mouth full of food. "I picked out your white dress for you that I laid across the bed with your shoes, socks, and slip." Granny said as she picked up my plate to wash it off. My grandma could not stand the sight of dishes been left in the sink. Taking my last bite, I said thanks and ran to my room to get dress. *I love my grandmother; I thought. She is the best.*

Putting my socks on, I heard the van pull up. "Come on Marti'ka." I heard my grandma yell from the living room. I guess I was tearing my grandma nerves up because this was the third time, she has yelled at me this morning. I put one shoe on, grabbed the other one and my children bible. I couldn't allow the van to wait on me any longer. I had to go.

Approaching the door, "Marti'ka if you don't put that other shoe on your foot. What have I told you about young ladies walking outside barefoot?" My grandma's morning was off because I didn't want to wake up this morning. I put my other shoe on my foot and ran out the door to embrace the beauty of the Sunday morning air. As the sun shined so bright, this day was about to be full of loves and laughers.

My grandma made sure that church was a part of our daily lives. She made sure that we learned about Jesus and what He should mean to us. Jesus wasn't an option in our house. He was mandatory.

5.5: The Perfect Remedy

Proverbs 22:6 states, "Train up a child in the way he should go, even when he is old, he will not depart from it." As children to adulthood, we are taught the things that we should do to help make our lives better. We are taught to listen and make correct choices in life. Proverbs 8:10 read, "Receive my instructions, and not silver; and knowledge rather than choice gold." To make choices that would avoid having a bad consequence after it. Yet, we are always giving a command to follow but are not always sure about the choice giving. Let's look at the definition of choice:

- the act of choosing.
- the act of picking or deciding between two or more possibilities.
- the opportunity or power to choose between two or more possibilities.
- a range of things that can be chosen.

Looking at the definition choice give you the option of more than one. So, when you are given a choice that you know may not product a positive result. I suggest you make a wiser decision, but only you can make the decision. So, it's really what to you!

5.6: I Need Jesus

The best choice I ever made was building a relationship with God. This relationship has helped me in many ways. Perhaps most importantly, it allowed me to see and understand the invisible battles I was waging. We don't fight against mere flesh and blood but against spirits in high places (Ephesians 6:12). Because of this, I strive to never judge how others live. And I hope that, as you read this section, you will keep an open mind. All of us have different spirits we battle daily, and I am no exception.

Some spiritual battles come from chasing normal, natural desires in the wrong way. Most people desire love, romance, and one day a family of their own. For some, this can lead to having many relationships involving sex. Caught up in the search for love, you never realize how much you are giving away. After each failed relationship, the grip of the spirit of loneliness grows stronger and stronger.

Let's be honest: pretty much everyone has faced the spirit of loneliness, which usually always occurs in different forms. In my case, I felt unloved. I was of no importance. I settled for unhealthy relationships because I feared being alone. If I was alone, I might have found myself and learn all about the person God has called me to be. Running from God, I became a person full of pain who built walls to keep others away. All of this started even before I had my first boyfriend. It all began when my father left.

I felt in my heart that, if my daddy wasn't here with me, he didn't love me. I didn't see myself worthy of love. As I began a lifelong battle with the spirit of loneliness, I allowed myself to experience depression, attempts at suicide, a drug addiction, and leading to someone else trying to take my life. Battling loneliness opens doors to other spirits that I wasn't aware of, and for years, they hindered any possibility at a relationship with God.

Yet, God started revealing Himself to me. He showed me that Jesus' grace kept me, restored me, and set me free. He began to show me who I could become. Around the age of 22, I started my journey of building my relationship with God. I realized that after the hell I faced in life, God created me for something greater.

The only way you will find out who you are is through God. He created you, so He knows everything about you. He is the only one you need to fulfill your dreams, to find out who you are, and to find your purpose. Don't allow your whole life to pass you by before realizing that you need Jesus. You need Jesus in everything that you do, so do not be ashamed of Him. He is the only Way, the Truth, and the Light.

It doesn't matter how many things you accomplish on this earth. If your greatest accomplishment isn't building your relationship with God and truly becoming one of His children, then none of it matters. Without Him, your life will be full of misdirection and confusion as you battle spirits without ever really noticing their presence.

Before I began building my relationship with God, He protected me, even as I made some of the worst choices of my life. He protected me from harm, seen and unseen. He bought me to this day. God has always loved me and always will. The same applies to you.

I can't tell you what to do. I can only encourage you and share my story with you. I do not have all the answers, and I hope that everyone looks at me as a sinner who knows she sins and falls short of God's glory every day. However, I am striving to hear "Well done, my good and faithful servant," and I believe that with Jesus all things are possible. My life changed with one good choice, and so can yours.

I learned that I had to allow God to be God in my life. I had to move my own fears and desires out of the way to find Him and find myself. Stop looking back at your past and who you used to be and look at your future and who God has called you to be.

5.7: Woman After God's Heart

It was June 2015 and I had just enrolled into Styletrends Academy. I was starting in the beginner class with two other people where I met a special woman name Mekia. Over the 6 weeks' time frame I was there, we made a bond that I cannot explain, nor did I understand it either.

When we met, I was in an exciting place in my life with God. I was building my relationship with Him and He was showing me things I never seem before.

Mekia was a real down to earth Christian woman. She always kept it real with me rather I liked it or not. Even though she would be talking to me she really wasn't talking to me. She was talking to my spirit because her spirit knew my spirit.

Now Mekia was not from Rock Hill. In fact, she moved and left everything after God's heart. She reminds me of Ruth from the bible. Ruth left everything that was known to her to follow her mother-in-law but honestly it was the God of Israel that she fell in love with.

Throughout school and even after graduating Mekia would always encourage me, cut-throat nicely with the word of God. Meaning, I would always hear the truth of God and reminded that my flesh can't win.

One day, we were talking, and I told her know why I stopped doing certain things. She responded, "So you are telling me just because something not going right you stop. You just give up because you battling with something? If you know God has called you to ministry, you must learn to stand even during your storm. That will make your testimony even stronger."

Saying a mouth full in so little words, I could not respond back to that. I knew that she was right and as much as I did not want to admit it, I had no choice but too. I had given up on somethings that I love and was helpful towards other because I couldn't get out my way.

Meeting Mekia lets me know that I must get out my own way. How can I expect God to take me higher if I cannot stand in the storm? How can I be promoted if I cannot function outside my comfort zone? If God can relocate her and provide her every need, then He can do it for me. She showed me what it was like to move out her way and start over. Letting me know that the journey will not be easy but well worth it. Letting me know that she is a woman after God's heart.

Sometimes the familiar areas are the area that keeps you bound. Yet, God will connect you with someone that can show you what you pray for. I know that been a woman after God's heart has been a prayer for me and through Mekia I am learning how to be.

God know your heart, your motives, and intentions. It is up to you and how you play your cards but be wise and careful. The wrong step can take a twist or turn in your faith.

5.8: Giving Should Be Natural

Giving sometimes is not an easy topic to discuss because we worry if our giving will be in vain. We are taught to give from the goodness of our heart and seek nothing in return. Soon, either finding out if our giving was purposeful or in vain So what is the definition of giving? Giving is:

-freely transfer the possession of (something) to (someone), hand over to.

-cause or allow (someone or something) to have (something, especially something abstract).

Now there are times when people will try to take advantage of your giving heart, but we should not withhold good from those to whom it is due, when it is in your power to do it (Proverbs 3:27).

I remember when I was working at Wal-Mart in the Photo Center and a young girl and her mother came in there to print some pictures. I am not sure how we got on the topic of her becoming a mother, but I soon found out she was just like me. A young single teenage mother.

She goes on to tell me about her child father not being active and all she had was her mother. She did not really have a lot of items for the baby, and she could use as much help as possible. My oldest baby had outgrown his stroller and a few other things. I told her that she could have what my baby no longer used.

I got her number, went home to collect those items, and I gave them to her a few days later. I gave those things to her without a doubt in my mind. Even though I was a young single mother myself, I could relate to her story.

I trust in my heart if I were to have another child that God would provide because I was giving to someone else in need. And a few years later when I got pregnant with my second baby, God had a family to bless my baby with a brand-new stroller and car seat set.

Giving to others shows the growth within you; you improve by taking the chance to help someone else. And often giving will give you a never-ending feeling that is unmistakable. Are you willing to give generously to someone who really needs your help?

5.9: I Can Help Them

One day I went to Dollar General to pick up a few items. Standing in line to check out behind me were a lady and her daughter. The lady, around fifty, was dressed in dirty, holey jeans and a faded black shirt, while her daughter, near twenty, wore similarly simple clothes. I overheard the lady telling her daughter that she was very tired, and they had a long walk to get home.

Feeling the pain that was running through the lady's body as if it were my own, I turned around and offered them a ride home. Readily they accepted. I checked out and walked outside to pack my car as I waited for them.

After almost five minutes of waiting, I walked back in to check on them only to see the lady counting out coins to pay for her items. She looked up at me, saying she was coming as she pushed the coins over to the cashier and grabbed her bags.

My heart was hurting as we walked outside. If only I could give them something more than just a ride, I thought. If only I was rich, I could really make a difference.

As they got into the car, the lady thanked me for the ride. She said that she was exhausted, and although she was not in any shape for that walk home, she would have done it if necessary. She also mentioned she just spent all she had to put a few items in the house that were needed. I nodded my head in understanding; I knew the feeling of spending your last for the things you need.

As I drove out of the parking lot, in my spirit I heard: "Turn back around, pay for her items, and give her money back to her." I can't lie and say I didn't question what He was telling me to do, but I decided to do it anyways. Not sure what I had got myself into, I turned back and poked my head in the store's door. The lines were still long like before; it would take too much time to pay for her purchase and get her money back.

Feeling confused, I got back in the car when I heard again in my spirit: "Go to the ATM and give her $20." Now, I need you to understand that I only had $40 in my bank account, including checking and savings. So now I hesitated, thinking, *God, all I got is $40!* However, in the end I did it anyways. I drove to the ATM across the street and took out $20.

Still not sure what God was up too, I handed the money to the lady. She just looked at me, confused. I told her it was something to help her out until she got some extra money. $20 may not be great deal of money, but it means a lot when you don't have anything at all. Hesitant to grab the money, she asked if I was sure before putting the money into her small bag.

After thanking me again, she started talking about her house, especially the chickens she had. The distance to her home in the car was only about 7 to 8 minutes but walking it would have been near 30 minutes to an hour. Soon, I was turning onto Blackmon Road, a long street where the homeless and less fortune in town live. As we kept driving, the pavement turned into a dirt road.

After turning right onto an uneven, narrow path, we came to a cluster of five wooden, shack-sized houses. I looked around, shocked at the homes, realizing just how blessed I truly was. The lady pointed out her home as the furthest little house. There were several chicken coops, with plenty of chickens running around outside.

For the next ten minutes, the lady and her daughter chatted with me. Telling me about their home, the grandchild, and their everyday struggles. Still talking with a smile and a peace that God would make everything already.

Shortly, saying goodbye, I slowly drove back down the rough, dusty roads. I gave God thanks for my encounter. I also began to pray that God would help me take care of my car, because it was not just for me but also for others in need.

Later that week, my neighbor asked me for a ride. I agreed but I let her know that I needed to get some gas while we were out. When she got in the car, she handled me $40 for gas. I looked at the money then looked at her, asking "Why so much?" She just told me to not worry about it and thanked me for the ride.

At first, I could hardly believe it, but then God reminded me what I did for that lady a few days ago. I gave her half of what I had, and God gave me back double. I trusted that God would support and enable me to do whatever He needs me to do. I moved in obedience, and He gave me a double portion.

There are times in life when you miss out on your blessings. The smallest blessing given in an act of generosity can make the biggest difference in the end. If God laid it on your heart to give to someone, obey the call and watch what God can do.

Having a giving spirit is like having a savings account that is never empty. If you give openly and from the heart, God will continually give back to you. There will be nothing lacking, and blessings, big and small, will continue to come, overflowing from your life and into the lives of those around you. Be willing to give and receive the blessings only God can bestow!

5.10: Forgiveness

Forgiveness can be a very touchy topic to speak on because sometimes we feel people don't deserve forgiveness from us. Yet, we want God to bless us abundantly without first forgiving others. So, what is the definition of forgiveness:

Forgiveness is the action of process of forgiving or being forgiven.

According to Matthew 6:14-15, "For if you forgive other people when they sin against you, your heavenly Father will also forgive you. But if you do not forgive others their sins, your Father will not forgive your sins.

If I asked you, have you ever been hurt before in your life, I already know that your answer will be yes. Some point in our lives we experience a hurt that makes it hard to bounce back. It makes it hard to truly recover that you allow more hurt to welcome itself in. Allowing more hurt to pile up on top of the hurt that was already there. Making it hard to regain your true strength to fight back. To stand. To conquer.

You hold on to something that is long and gone. You can't take it back. It can't be replaced. Yet, you still hold on but why? Because it changed your life forever? It put a hole in your heart. It made you question you without truly experiencing love and happiness? Walking around with a wall up against those that hurt you and not even giving anyone else the chance to know you.

I encourage you to forgive and let go. To forgive those that hurt you, to forgive yourself, and mostly importantly God. Walking with un-forgiveness in your heart is like poison to the body. Slowly creeping in your bloodstream, traveling to every part of your body killing everything within you, from the inside to the out.

I held on to the pain of those who hurt me for a long time. I just couldn't let go and I didn't understand why not. Holding on caused me to lose sight of myself along the years. I fought every day, only to realize that my fighting was getting worst.

I had to realize that I had to let go. I had to forgive. I went from trying to commit suicide to someone trying to kill me. I allowed myself to settle in life with certain things instead of growing. Those un-forgiveness marks were holding me down. I had to learn to truly shake them off.

Over time as they fell off, it felt like I had lost 1,000 pounds off my shoulders. My shoulders were no longer full of the worries of yesterday. I realized the pain other people caused helped to push me towards my destiny. I was now able to truly look ahead.

Forgiveness isn't for the person that hurt you but for you. Forgiveness allows you to be free, so you can live and enjoy life. Your breakthrough depends on your level of forgiveness. Do not allow your entire life to pass you by because you refuse to forgive. Forgive, love, and laugh so you can live.

5.11: *JESUS Can Do It All*

During the time I was going through everything in life when I didn't have anyone to depend on, Jesus was always there. Growing up as a child, I never understood the importance of who Jesus Christ really was but as I matured, I realized I need Him in everything that I do.

Who exactly is Jesus Christ some may ask? Well, He is God's only begotten son. He is the Messiah sent by God to save humans from sin, which it inherited through the fall of man.

God our Father sent Jesus to save us from our sins and to give us a chance at everlasting life. John 14:6 states "Jesus saith unto him, I am the way, the truth, and the life: no man cometh unto the Father, but by me." He provides a strong, just, and everlasting love for everyone to experience and share with others.

Regardless, if we want to accept it or not Jesus holds ALL power in His hand. In Him will we find the treasures of wisdom and knowledge (Colossians 2:3) (KJV). Even in prayer, if two or more are gathered together, He will be in the mist of it (Matthew 18:20) (KJV).

Jesus has a unique significance in the world that no prophet, spiritual leader, or philosopher can rival. He was conceived by the Holy Spirit in a virgin named Mary. Unlike Adam, who was created without sin but eventually fell. Jesus never sinned against God during his 33 years on earth. He performed wonderful miracles and introduced the truth of God to the world. Jesus died on the cross for our sins and transgressions. Three days later He rose again so that we may have life. He loved us so much that He died to save those who believe in Him. Even though Jesus ascended into heaven, He left us with the Holy Spirit to guide us along our way while we journey along this earth.

I can tell you from experience that Jesus has changed me from the worst the best. Even though it has all been a process, it was Jesus that did it all. I encourage you to learn about Him and build a relationship with Him. Learn to call on the name of Jesus and watch how His name alone can move a mountain. Never be afraid to trust Him or to call on His name!

Jesus loves you! He loves us all because the love of God flows through Him. Taste and see that the Lord is good (Psalm 34:8) (KJV).

5.12: Acceptance

After I sit back and reflect over 31 years of my life, I realize that I have been fighting for acceptance from others. In some form or another, I was seeking acceptance because I felt I needed that surety from someone else. I didn't truly take the time to love me. To accept Marti'ka for Marti'ka because I was always searching to fill a void. A void that only God could fill.

I had to accept me and love on Marti'ka, which was kind of hard because I have always tried to love others before myself.

Regardless of every storm from my childhood to now, I promised myself that I would forever accept and love me. No longer looking for man to love me but to accept God's love, my boys, and family but most importantly self-love. So, in acceptance of loving Marti'ka I made myself a decree, just for me.

5.13: A Queen's Decree

I am created in the image of God

I am fearfully and wonderfully made

I am the daughter of a King

The Most High

I will no longer settle for less then I deserve

And I deserve everything

My Father desires for me to have

No doubt No fear

I forgive and let go

For my future is in tomorrow

Oh Lord, change my thoughts

More about You

Guide my footsteps

Control my tongue

Bless me with wisdom, knowledge, and understanding

Protect and hide me oh Lord

Strength to love me

Courage to stand

Hope to achieve

Faith to believe

No longer looking backwards

Looking only ahead

Shining bright

Like the diamond I am

Beautiful just like a gorgeous jewel

Yes, that's me

This is my decree

To faithfully love me

    I have accepted my choices of my past so I can move forward in my life. As much as I fought to hold on to some things, I no longer could handle it. I was missing life for not even truly loving me. So, I encourage you to accept it all, forgive and move on. Tomorrow isn't promising to hold on to yesterday.

Conclusion

As this book ends, I encourage you to break those pieces in your life that may be hindering you from being the best you. Is it an easy battle to fight. NO! Worth it in the end? YES! Say goodbye to those broken pieces. Allow God to pick them up and put them back together. His way is way better than our way.

I don't know everything. I don't have all the answers. I can only share with you my past, my life, my stories. Some battles I faced in life some people could never face them, but other people battle I could not face.

You have your own unique story. Rather you like it or not. It's yours'! So, I encourage you to face it, embrace it, and OWN it! Change does not come over night. There is a process that you must go through, but ultimately you can accomplish whatever you set your mind to do.

Take time to reflect on yourself and who you are. Learn who God has called you to be. Take back control of your mind and body and truly live. So, as I come to my final goodbyes, I would like to leave you with this:

-Build a true relationship with JESUS.

-Form a constant PRAYER life.

-Remember GIVING is a blessing.

-Believe in your DREAMS.

-Strive to make CORRECT choices.

-Learn from your WRONG choices.

-Walk with COURAGE to overcome all things.

-DEDICATE yourself to God's will.

-Chose SUCCESS in your life.

-Most importantly, ACCEPT who you are.

You can't do anything about the past, but you can do something about your future. Never be afraid to break the chains on those broken pieces in order to chase your dream so you can walk into your future. Speak it into existence. Claim it! Conquer it! I encourage you to do it. Go for it! Aim towards the sky!

Life will most definitely throw you curve balls, but the secret to win is Christ Jesus. We are all winners in Christ Jesus to those that believe. In every battle that you may face, know that with Christ Jesus ALL things are possible (Philippians 4:13).

Are you living or are you existing?

I love you and God bless!

My Special Prayer

Dear Father,

As I come to You in need of prayer, I ask that You please forgive me of my sins. Forgive me for those I may have hurt and forgive those who may have hurt me and others as well. Father, thank you for everything that You have done, are doing, and will continue to do. Please help me, Father, and guide me through this day and throughout the rest of my life.

Humble me, oh Lord! Help me to control my tongue and change any negative thoughts, words, and actions into positive, uplifting thoughts, words, and actions. I can no longer fight this war here on earth alone. I know that You will never leave me nor forsake me.

Due to Jeremiah 29:11, I know that You have a purpose for me here on this earth. Continue to love, mold, teach, guide, comfort, and provide, and never leave my side. I am sorry if I am not the child that You want me to be, but I am growing and maturing into the child Your heart desires.

As I continue along my journey, please continue to help me. What is it that you have for me? Where do I go from here? How do I achieve my accomplishments? I pray for peace, love, and happiness but also guidance along the way. Control my mind, thoughts, actions, and words.

Thank you, my Father and God, for everything that You do, with love, understanding, and thanksgiving. In Jesus' name I pray! Amen. Amen. Amen.

With much love from a child with a broken heart, searching for love and righteousness.

Each prayer takes you closer to your dreams. Never stop believing in yourself and ALWAYS have faith in God! I love you and I pray as you start to pick up those broken pieces, that you can find yourself and become whole!

www.ingramcontent.com/pod-product-compliance
Lightning Source LLC
Chambersburg PA
CBHW050636160426
43194CB00010B/1697